INTERNATIONAL BANKING

INTERNATIONAL BANKING

The foreign activities of the banks of
principal industrial countries

Ursel Steuber

A. W. Sijthoff — Leyden-1976

497712

A publication of the
HWWA-Institut für Wirtschaftsforschung, Hamburg

Translated by Rita and Robin Pringle, London, from:
Internationale Banken, Auslandsaktivitäten von Banken bedeutender Industrieländer,
published by Verlag Weltarchiv GmbH, Hamburg, 1974

HG
3881
.S74313
1976

ISBN 90 286 0375 1

Printed in The Netherlands

PREFACE

The internationalisation of corporate business activities by means of foreign direct investment — the establishment of facilities of production or distribution abroad — grew rapidly in the 1960s. The leaders in this development, which has given a new dimension to the world division of labour, were the large American companies, whose endeavours were spurred by the formation of the EEC. European and Japanese firms, which had hitherto served the world market by exporting directly to their overseas customers, followed suit. Since then the process has speeded up, and has acquired a dynamic of its own. The economic, social and political consequences of this world-wide investment activity and of the related emergence of multinational enterprises have only begun to be recognised and assessed. The HWWA-Institut für Wirtschaftsforschung-Hamburg, supported by the German Research Society (special research area 86), is currently investigating the extent, characteristics and effects of direct investments and multinational enterprises on the participating countries' economies and on the world economic system.

This is the context of the following study of the internationalisation process in the field of banking. Banks were somewhat tardy in following the trend towards the establishment of direct bases abroad. Again it was American institutions who were the first to take the initiative after the war. Today the business philosophy of major banks in all industrial countries is international and their cross-frontier expansion is continuing rapidly. The organisational form of these foreign activities is constantly changing; likewise, the business possibilities offered by them are characterised by a constant extension and specialisation. For example, the formation of centres whose boundaries were at first limited to one region has generally given way to a global orientation. This development, induced by the large and growing demand for international financing and investment services, carried forward by the wealth of invention and the activity of bankers, is extremely important for the world economy. It raises new tasks for international economic policy — problems which can only be solved in co-operation.

The present investigation will, we trust, help to clarify this process of internationalisation. For the first time it supplies a complete comparative survey of the foreign operations of major banks in five significant industrial countries: the United States, Great Britain, the Federal Republic of Germany, France and Japan. The study analyses firstly the methods, the extent and the regional structure of the business activities of these banks abroad and, secondly, the preferred regions and financial centres in which they have invested. The appendix gives details of the foreign activities of significant credit institutions and specifies the most important international consortium banks. As aggregate statistics were only rarely available, numerous individual references and sources had to be employed and combined; naturally in this respect the author benefited from her access to the files of the HWWA Institute. This attention to detail gives, in our opinion, a particular value to the investigation. However, herein also lie its limits. By necessity a high level of description is all that could be aimed at rather than a comprehensive analytical work. The Institute and the author would therefore be very grateful for any comments or additional complementary information that readers feel able to supply. This would also be of assistance for further investigations in future.

The book was first published in German by Verlag Weltarchiv GmbH, Hamburg. The present English edition has been updated, and a special annex on the foreign activities of major US banks has been added. In order to help readers keep up to date about current developments in the field of international banking the Institute is planning to publish from time to time supplements to the book. Readers who wish to be kept informed about these publications are kindly asked to send the request form on the last page of this volume to the HWWA Institute.

Many representatives of credit institutions abroad and at home have made available information for this study and advised the author in her work. Our gratitude to them is great. Finally, we wish to express our deep appreciation to Rita and Robin Pringle for their great endeavours and skills in translating the German text into excellent English. Of course, for all errors and shortcomings only the author and the Institute are responsible.

Hans-Eckart Scharrer
Hamburg,   *International Monetary*
August 1975   *Policies Department*

CONTENTS

X

SURVEY OF TABLES

XI

APPENDICES

.

1

INTERNATIONALISATION IN BANKING

With the increasing economic integration of Western economies, as manifested in the growth of trading links and also of direct investment,[1] a strong trend towards internationalisation in the banking sector too is a natural development. However, while overseas direct investments by industrial enterprises have played an important role for a long time, banking has begun to change, fundamentally, only in the last ten years. Up to the early 1960s correspondent bank relationships were the predominant method of conducting foreign business. Only after then did banks emerge strongly as foreign investors. Their growing involvement in international activity was evidenced in a rapid expansion of foreign branch networks, in the foundation and enlargement of participations in affiliated companies abroad for the execution of special banking business as well as in the establishment of co-operative joint ventures with banks from various countries. This resulted in the development of multinational banks, i.e. banks with branch networks and/or subsidiaries or participations in companies in several countries.

This change in the direction of business policy in the banking sector took place for several reasons. The growth of industrial enterprises far beyond national borders, the movement towards larger corporate units by way of mergers or take-overs, and the emergence of large multinational enterprises brought about a far-reaching change — both quantitative and qualitative — in the nature of the demands made on banks and the services required of them.

The quantitative aspect is a reflection of the increasing financial requirements of industrial enterprises. This in turn results from the increase in investment activity and in the capital intensity of investment. Because of the lower ratio of self-financing, companies' own resources have not been sufficient to finance the new investments, and so a large part of the capital required has had to be provided by external sources, with a large share taken by loans. As national markets were often unable to provide a supply of finance corresponding to the demand for it and as controls on capital transactions also often barred companies from access to domestic markets, multinational enterprises financed themselves increasingly on the capital markets of various countries. In view of this increasing internationalisation, banks also became convinced of the need to widen their activities far beyond the narrow confines of national frontiers, in order to do justice to the big change in the quantitative demands made on them.

The qualitative change in the demands made on banks also resulted partly from the increase in companies' direct investment abroad. In order to be in a position to offer a wide range of services in as many parts of the world as possible, including consultancy as well as financial advisory services, banks realised they had to be represented abroad. But even apart from those international companies, others which were not in the least multinational in character and were not even intending to make overseas direct investments also expected much more from their banks than the customary services offered to them. For example, they would frequently need a comprehensive consultancy and information service about foreign markets and sales outlets as well as on possible partners for co-operative ventures, participation agreements, merger possibilities and so forth.

The changed pattern of demand was met at first primarily by the American banks, which established world-wide branch networks. The focus was in Europe, where US investment was concentrated. A further spur to international activities, notably on the Euro-currency and Euro-bond markets, was provided by the introduction of the Interest Equalisation Tax and the various programmes for improving the US balance of payments. After the first of these, in 1967, American corporations had to procure the long-term capital required for their overseas investments increasingly from off-shore sources. Suddenly, a large extra demand was transferred to the European markets.

Along with the changed demand situation, American competition played a decisive role in sparking off the extension of European banks' international activities. In addition, the growth of the Euro-markets and the increasing need felt by industrial companies to tap these markets as sources of finance were further factors making it necessary for banks to secure, if possible, direct access to these markets. The Euro-dollar market has indeed contributed greatly to the overall expansion of bank credit, as is made clear by looking at its explosive growth in recent years. Thus it was through this much greater competition on both sides of the balance sheet, so to speak, both for sources of funds and in the provision of financial services, that the internationalisation of banking was pushed rapidly forward.

2

DIFFERENT FORMS
OF INTERNATIONAL ACTIVITY

The business activities which banks carry out beyond national borders can be conducted in various ways. In choosing between them, various different variables may have an influence – for example legislative requirements in the foreign country concerned and/or in the home country, or the individual business objectives of the bank concerned. Its business policy is dependent essentially upon how deeply its existing customers are committed abroad and how great the possibilities are of gaining new customers in the country in which the investment is to take place. For carrying out their international business, banks have the choice of the following types of representation:

– Correspondent bank connections
– Representative offices
– Participations
– Subsidiary companies
– Branch establishments
– Joint ventures

The traditional type of *correspondent bank* connection lost its significance with the banks' growing interest in the expansion of their foreign business. Normally the settlement of payments transactions arising from foreign trade is made to a large extent by correspondent banks even after the opening of a direct establishment by the "home" bank. This way of carrying out foreign business will not be considered

5

further here, because correspondent bank business depends on the demand situation and a correspondent bank connection does not represent a direct investment abroad in the sense that a participation or a branch abroad does, for example.

A *representative office* serves as a point of contact with enterprises abroad, facilitates the establishment of new business connections and may open up or deepen sources of information. As the representative office itself does not carry out banking business, clients have to be passed on to local banks or to branches of third country banks. Whilst being complementary to a correspondent bank connection, a representative office can represent a home bank's interests better than can a correspondent bank. In addition, its existence can prove very useful if the opening of a branch is planned for a later date.

Taking a *participation* in an existing or legally independent credit or finance institution abroad enables a bank to enlarge the services it can itself offer and to improve its market position. The acquisition of participations in specialised institutions, for instance in leasing, factoring, or investment companies are especially suitable for a bank wishing to diversify its services. In comparison with establishing branches, participations can be taken on a smaller input of capital.

From the point of view of capital costs, the establishment of *foreign subsidiaries* are very similar to the acquisition of a majority participation. But in contrast to the latter, a subsidiary will have a definitely foreign character, and this will influence business activity in various ways, depending on the country concerned. Subsidiaries abroad have their own legal personality and are often founded for special tasks which the head office cannot carry out from its home base. The type of business activity conducted by subsidiaries can frequently be surmised from the country, i.e. the financial centre – for example in Luxembourg or the Bahamas – where they are established.

Foreign branches do not have their own legal identity, and are, in the organisational sense, an integral part of the bank itself. For the customer it is a great advantage if he can complete all his financial business through the foreign branch network of his own domestic bank. While American banks, in particular, built up a world-wide network of branches, German banks (to take the instance of Germany here) were very hesitant in making this type of commitment abroad.

In considering the forms of direct office establishments of foreign banks in the United States two types have to be distinguished: branches and agencies. They differ with regard to the range of business activity conducted. Agencies are not allowed to accept deposits. They can only do business on the assets side of their balance sheet, for which they must find the necessary resources from their parent banks, from the money markets and/or from other banks. A branch, however, can carry out practically all banking business. In making the choice between them the business policy of the parent institution is clearly decisive; that is to say, it depends on whether the foreign bank in America wants only to do lending business, or if it also sees an opportunity for gaining deposit accounts on the American market.

Joint ventures on a co-operative basis between banks — mostly from different countries — have attained much significance, especially for European banks, as a way of carrying out their international business. According to the usage of the English language they can also be called consortium banks. The often used concept "multinational bank" for joint ventures does not seem suitable in so far as the phrase is here applied just to the multinational composition of the shareholders. A true multinational bank should rather be analogous to the concept "multinational enterprise" in the industrial field, i.e. comprise those banks which maintain branches and/or subsidiary and affiliated companies in several countries. This institutionalised cross-frontier co-operation, where each one of the participating banks retains intact its independent decision-making capacity, seems to be for many banks the only possibility of attaining an economically optimal scale of activities in international business, because this way of expanding international activities demands a relatively small input of long-term investments on behalf of the individual associated bank. It opens numerous possibilities for diversification and for a flexible adjustment to changing market conditions. Besides in this way the

7

foreign branches of the individual banks contribute to the extension of the territorial business coverage of all the participants – both on the assets and liabilities sides of their balance sheets. Disadvantages of this method might be seen in the pooling of the business possibilities and profits as well as in the problems that arise through the voting of the partners as regards the business policy to be followed.

The main function of a number of the largest and most important multibank enterprises consists in carrying out medium and long-term credit business on the Euro-dollar market. Besides these companies are engaged in other Euro-dollar business, including short-term money market operations. Some of them also undertake other normal banking transactions. They are purely commercial banks, in which several independent banks participate as partners.

The institutional channels for conducting foreign activity described here are used by most banks in parallel to each other. But the banking groups of the various countries frequently show a preference for certain ways rather than others for conducting their international business. This can be seen from the following chapter.

3

EXTENT AND STRUCTURE OF
THE FOREIGN ACTIVITIES OF THE BANKS
OF PRINCIPAL INDUSTRIAL COUNTRIES

3.1. American banks abroad

a) *Special features of the American banking system* [2]

In the United States a test of need is required for the founding of new commercial banks as well for the establishment of new branches. According to the prevailing American laws on branching, an interstate construction of branch networks – as for instance exists in European countries – is not allowed. Subsidiaries can only be founded within the boundaries of the State in which the bank concerned has its head office, and here mostly within confined limits. Apart from the boundaries set to the physical expansion of banks there are also restrictions on their business policy. The range of services a bank can offer essentially corresponds to that of a universal bank, but stock exchange business and the underwriting of securities is not permitted. Furthermore the commercial banks are restricted in their pricing policy by regulation Q, which determines the maximum interest rates they can offer.[3]

Because of the restrictions on branching, the physical expansion of American banks has taken place mainly through the instrument of the Bank Holding Company. The special type known as the One-Bank Holding Company was preferred, the subsidiary companies of which could, up to the Bank Holding Company Amendment Act in 1970, carry out every kind of business in every town in the United

States—including non-bank business. After that time the business activities of bank holding companies have been amended to cover bank and bank-related activities only. Through the non-bank subsidiary company of its holding company, which can be established nationwide in the United States, it is possible for the banks to carry out every bank-related business in the whole area of the United States. But growing expansion of the commercial banks shows itself not only inside America, but also in their greater international commitment.

In the expansion of their international activities the foreign branch establishment of American banks played, up to the end of the fifties, only a secondary part. During the period from 1951 to 1961 the number of foreign branches of American banks only increased from 100 to 135. For the carrying out of their transactions the banks with a large-scale foreign business preferred to rely on their world-wide extensive correspondent bank networks. In the first half of the 1960s only the First National City Bank (FNCB) disposed of a large number of branches abroad.[4] Of 180 branches abroad open in 1964, by 11 American banks, 100 were operated by the FNCB, 29 by the Chase Manhattan and 24 by the Bank of America.[5] By reason of the strong growth of foreign direct investments by US industrial enterprises and their financial requirements, the American commercial banks pushed strongly ahead with their foreign commitments during the second half of the 1960s.[6] This was further strengthened by the American controls on capital transactions which made it difficult for the enterprises to obtain capital in the United States. The greatest expansion took the form of the setting-up of foreign branches. In addition, they founded a number of subsidiary companies, acquired numerous participations in foreign banks and, to a lesser extent, established joint enterprises together with other banks.

b) *Extent and regional distribution of the business activity of foreign branches*

In connection with the intense activity of American banking, the dynamic development of its foreign network of branches speaks for itself. From end 1965 to end 1973 the number of foreign branches trebled from 211 to about 650 (see Table 1). The expansion is shown even more clearly in the balance-sheet totals, which during the same period grew from $9,102 millions to $121,866 millions (see Table 1). Leaving aside the exceptional explosian in the balance-sheet total in the year 1969 (of 78.6 per cent), total assets have increased on average by about 30 per cent per annum. The extraordinarily steep increase in the year 1969 in the main resulted from the restrictive credit policy followed in the United States and the related high level of refinancing of US Banks head offices by their foreign branches.

Table 1. Number and total assets of US banks' foreign branches, 1965-73

	Number of US banks' foreign branches	Total assets ($ millions)	Increase in total assets (%) compared with the previous year
1965	211	9,102	–
1966	244	12,384	36.1
1967	295	15,658	26.4
1968	375	23,018	47.0
1969	459	41,120	78.6
1970	536	52,611	27.9
1971	577	67,054	27.5
1972	627	77,437	15.5
1973	ca 650	121,866[a]	

Note
a. *Federal Reserve Bulletin,* Vol. 61, No. 1 (January 1975) p. A72.

Sources
U.S. Banks' Branches Overseas: A Statistical Record, 1965-1969, An annual compilation by the Federal Reserve Board, in *The Journal of Commerce,* New York, No. 22338 (December 14, 1970). U.S. Banking Overseas, in *The Journal of Commerce,* New York, No. 23091 (December 10, 1973), and the author's calculations.

The rapid expansion of foreign branches and their business activity reflects not only the fast growth of the large international US banks but also the increasing participation of medium and smaller-sized banks in international banking. Altogether about 130 banks were represented abroad in 1974.[7]

As regards the regional distribution of branches abroad (see Table 2) the Latin American countries dominate in terms of numbers. This is conditioned by historical circumstances. Already in 1965 there were in existence 88 foreign branches in Latin America and by the end of 1971 229 were open. After 1968 offices in continental Europe and Great Britain took second place, before these in the Far East. With regard to the increase in branches continental Europe shows the largest rate of increase. The strong representation of the US banks has been noticed for a few years in the Bahamas, where the number of branches increased between 1969 and 1972 from 31 to 94.

Table 2. Regional distribution of US banks' foreign branches, 1965-72

	1965	1966	1967	1968	1969	1970	1971	1972
Great Britain and Ireland	22	22	25	35	40	44	48	53
Continental Europe	21	26	34	46	64	72	80	89
Latin America	88	102	133	178	203	223	229	227
The Bahamas	–	–	–	–	31	61	73	94
The Near East and Africa	–	–	–	–	7	14	17	17
The Far East	50	57	63	72	76	79	83	97
US overseas regions and trust territories	23	29	31	35	38	43	47	50
Other areas	7	8	9	9	–	–	–	–
Total	211	244	295	375	459	536	577	627

Sources
U.S. Banks' Branches Overseas: A Statistical Record, 1965-1969, An annual compilation by the Federal Reserve Board, in *The Journal of Commerce,* New York, No. 22338 (December 14, 1970). U.S. Banking Overseas, in *The Journal of Commerce,* New York, No. 23091 (December 10, 1973).

The regional distribution of the number of foreign branches however does not give any indication of the amount of the balance-sheet totals in various countries or country groups and for that reason does not permit statements about its significance for banks in the country of investment nor for the institutions from the countries of origin. If the balance-sheet total of the foreign branches is considered in terms of its development by region, the branches located in European countries – apart from Great Britain – are in the foreground (see Table 3). The US banks thereby followed the trend of direct investments by American industrial enterprises, which recorded the highest rate of increase in Europe in the years 1960 to 1970.[8] On average during the years 1965 to 1972 the assets of branches in Europe accounted for about 70 per cent of the total assets of US banks' foreign branches and on average approx. 53 per cent was contributed by branches in Great Britain (including Ireland). The strong position of Great Britian points to London's dominating position as an international financial centre for foreign bank branches. The largest increase took place in 1969, when the total assets of the American foreign branches in Great Britain increased by approx. 88 per cent to $24,753 millions and in continental Europe by approx. 57 per cent to $6,464 millions which in total corresponds to a share of 76 per cent of the total assets of all foreign branches. The annual rate of increase of the balance-sheet totals of the European branches clearly slowed down in the years 1970 and 1971, whereby, by contrast with the previous years, a stronger growth can be noticed at the continental European branches than at the British branches (see Table 4). Then in 1972 the growth rates fell sharply. This was especially marked at the continental European branches where total assets rose by only 0.9 per cent, i.e. were virtually stagnant. The relative share in the total assets of all foreign branches during the period from 1965 to 1972 taken by the region of Latin America fell from 9 per cent to 3 per cent and that of the Far East fell from 19 per cent to 9 per cent though total assets in the Far East increased strongly, especially during the years 1970 and 1971. In Latin America, however, they decreased despite the setting up of many new branches and since 1970 the rate of growth has been low. Against this, branches in the Bahamas increased their share in the total assets of US banks' branches abroad in only four years (1969-1972) from 7 per cent to 15 per cent, recording a growth of about 48 per cent, 78 per cent and 48 per cent in the three years 1970, 1971 and 1972 respectively. The strong commitment of American banks in the Bahamas is attributable to tax advantages and low

Table 3. Growth of total assets of US banks' foreign branches, by region, 1965-72

	1965		1966		1967		1968		1969		1970		1971		1972	
	$ millions	%	$ millions	%	$ millions	%	$ millions	%	$ millions	%	$ millions	%	$ millions	%	$ millions	%
Great Britain and Ireland	4.270	47	6.445	52	8.178	52	13.177	57	24.753	60	29.668	57	35.143	52	40.914	53
Continental Europe	1.354	15	2.022	16	2.721	17	4.121	18	6.464	16	9.496	18	12.913	19	13.033	17
Latin America	878	9	1.052	9	1.270	8	1.736	7	1.584	4	2.055	4	2.519	4	2.602	3
The Bahamas	–	–	–	–	–	–	–	–	2.993	7	4.421	8	7.849	12	11.576	15
The Near East and Africa	–	–	–	–	–	–	–	–	265	1	315	1	384	1	386	1
The Far East	1.700	19	1.808	15	2.267	15	2.663	11	3.257	8	4.423	8	6.221	9	7.119	9
US overseas regions and trust territories	634	7	787	6	965	6	1.287	6	1.804	6	2.233	4	2.025	4	1.807	2
Other areas	266	3	270	2	257	2	284	2	–	–	–	–	–	–	–	–
Total	9.102	100	12.384	100	15.658	100	23.018	100	41.120	100	52.611	100	67.054	100	77.437	100

Sources
U.S. Banks' Branches Overseas: A Statistical Record, 1965-1969, An annual compilation by the Federal Reserve Board, in The Journal of Commerce, New York, No. 22338 (December 14, 1970). U.S. Banking Overseas, in The Journal of Commerce, New York, No. 23091 (December 10, 1973); and author's calculations.

Table 4. Annual growth rates of the assets of US banks' foreign branches, by region, 1966-72

(in %)

	1966	1967	1968	1969	1970	1971	1972
Great Britain and Ireland	50.9	26.9	61.1	87.9	19.9	18.5	16.4
Continental Europe	49.3	34.6	51.5	56.9	46.9	36.0	0.9
Latin America	19.8	20.7	36.7	-8.8	29.7	22.6	3.3
The Bahamas	–	–	–	–	47.7	77.5	47.5
The Near East and Africa	–	–	–	–	18.9	21.9	0.5
The Far East	6.4	25.4	17.5	22.3	35.8	40.7	14.4
US overseas regions and trust territories	24.1	22.6	33.4	40.2	23.8	-9.3	89.2
Other areas	1.5	-4.8	10.5	–	–	–	–
Total	36.1	26.4	47.0	78.6	27.9	27.5	15.5

Source
As for Table 3.

running expenses as well as the country's liberal legislation, which imposes no limitations on the banks' business activity.

c) *Structure of the business activities of foreign branches*

In the development of the balance-sheet totals of foreign branches, time deposits form the most important item amongst liabilities with a share of over 60 per cent. Until 1968 three quarters and since 1969 almost as much as 90 per cent of total deposits were held in time deposits. The increase in time deposits was attributable mainly to Euro-dollars. The most rapid increase occurred in 1969, when total volume increased to $30.4 billions and thereby almost tripled (see Table 5). By 1972 the volume had doubled again. On the side of assets the largest share is represented by loans which experienced their largest increase (one of 57 per cent) in 1970. While claims on US head offices expanded strongly until 1969 (in that year they rose by 134 per cent), their total amount has fallen away since then. Also noteworthy is the extensive growth in sight balances, which rose by 142 per cent in

1969, 70 per cent in 1970, 50 per cent in 1971 and 48 per cent in 1972, reflecting the intense activity of the foreign branches on the Euromoney markets, i.e. the placing of Euro-dollars on the inter-bank market.

Table 5. Selected balance-sheet items of US banks' foreign branches, 1965-72

(in $ millions)

	1965	1966	1967	1968	1969	1970	1971	1972
Sight balances	1.5	1.7	2.4	3.3	8.0	13.6	20.4	30.2
Loans	4.6	5.0	6.6	9.2	13.0	20.4	27.7	36.3
Claims on parent banks and branches	4.6	5.0	4.0	6.1	14.3	8.6	3.7	2.1
Time deposits	5.0	7.4	9.8	10.9	30.4	36.5	44.8	61.6
Total assets	9.1	12.4	15.7	23.0	41.1	52.6	67.1	77.4

Sources
U.S. Banks' Branches Overseas: A Statistical Record, 1965-1969, An annual compilation by the Federal Reserve Board, in *The Journal of Commerce,* New York, No. 22338 (December 14, 1970). U.S. Banking Overseas, in *The Journal of Commerce,* New York, No. 23091 (December 10, 1973). Die Präsenz der amerikanischen Banken im Ausland, in *Neue Zürcher Zeitung,* No. 286 (October 18, 1972).

With the growth of the Euro-dollar market and in connection with the American capital export controls as well as developments on the American money market, considerable changes took place in the sources of finance and in the credit structure of foreign branches. Until 1965 the *American head offices* appeared to only a small extent as borrowers from their foreign branches.[9] The granting of credit to them by their foreign branches moved ahead only in 1966 and 1969 because of the tough restrictive monetary policy enforced in the United States. Through the restriction on maximum interest rates on time deposits determined by the regulation Q, time deposit rates were held below the market interest rates on comparable money market instruments and below the rates which were available from finance institutions competing with the commercial banks. So they turned to

16

their foreign branches where they could obtain funds on more favourable conditions than in the United States. The refinancing of the US banks in this way took place above all in London. In order to curb the growing take-up of such credit, the Federal Reserve Board introduced in the autumn of 1969 a minimum reserve ratio of 10 per cent on net borrowing by head offices from foreign branches (with a minimum amount, free of reserve, of 3 per cent of the deposits). The indebtedness of the US banks to their foreign branches had indeed already reached its peak of $14.4 billions in 1969 (compare Table 5) when, as against the previous year, the net take-up of credit more than doubled.

When the situation on the American money markets eased in the following year, the demand by the US banks for Euro-dollar credits from their foreign branches diminished. The net take-up of credit fell in 1970 by 40 per cent to $8.6 billions; in 1971 it decreased by a further 57 per cent to $3.7 billions. The Federal Reserve Board at the beginning of 1971 had increased the minimum reserve ratio requirement for such foreign credit to 20 per cent. At the same time, with the decrease in lending to their head offices the foreign branches also recorded a fall in the rate of growth of deposits, i.e. they were not forced any longer to solicit deposits by offering especially attractive inducements.

Foreign banks have gained in significance as borrowers from American foreign branches, which had however at the same time limited access to non-bank sources of funds. Liabilities to foreign commercial banks rose to $19.5 billions in September 1969 and claims on foreign banks to $8 billions. Thus the net borrowings of the foreign branches from foreign commercial banks increased to $11.5 billions. In the following years such assets grew more rapidly than the liabilities; at end 1971 the volume of assets amounted to $24.6 billions and that of the liabilities to $31.1 billions. The decrease in the net borrowings from foreign commercial banks to $6.5 billions at end 1971 was clearly reflected in the decline in lending by foreign branches to their American parent banks and demonstrated that the corresponding financial resources were placed increasingly with foreign commercial banks.

The decrease in the flow of capital to US head offices and the decrease in interest rates on the Euro-dollar market favoured a strong increase in lending to non-banks. While the assets and liabilities of foreign branches vis-à-vis non banks were almost in balance until end-1969, net lendings to non-banks increased to $4.2 billions at end-1970, and to $9.0 billions at end-1971, thereby more than doubling. Total assets at end-1971 stood at $17.8 billions as against $11.6 billions in the previous year and that of the liabilities were $8.8 billions as against $7.4 billions. This increase can be ascribed, on the one hand, to the remarkable strength of the demand for credit by multinational enterprises and, on the other hand, to borrowings by American investors, who after 1965 had to finance their activities increasingly abroad at a time when the granting of credit by US banks abroad was limited by the Voluntary Foreign Credit Restraint Programme (VFCR). Also the Interest Equalisation Tax (IET), which had been made applicable to credits extended to foreign borrowers with a maturity of more than one year, as well as the regulations of the Foreign Direct Investment Programme, were working in the same direction.

d) *Subsidiaries, participations and co-operative ventures abroad*

The expansion of US banks abroad has taken place not only through the expansion of their foreign branch networks but also through the growing number of subsidiaries active abroad, the acquisition of participations (see Appendix 2) and the establishment of consortium banks, together with foreign banks (see Appendix 1). US banks can establish or acquire subsidiaries abroad or participations in foreign banks directly as well as through their Edge Act Corporations.[10]

Until 1967 this was possible only by means of the instrument of their Edge Act subsidiaries.[11] The number of these specialised institutions increased from 59 in 1967 to 70 in 1970 and to 89 in 1972.[12] The capital invested in these companies by American banks amounted to $640 millions in 1970. The Edge Act subsidiaires founded in New York functioned as the main servicing centres and connecting links between foreign branches and the US banks headquartered outside New York during the period of large Euro-dollar borrowing, which reached its climax in 1969.[13]

Also in recent years US banks have founded, just in London alone, 11 merchant banks, of which nine are 100 per cent owned, and two have a majority stake held by American banks [14] (see Table 6). Most of these subsidiaries have concentrated, apart from the aquisition of participations in foreign companies, on medium-term credit business and new issues and underwriting business. The acquisition of participations by foreign branches is not allowed.

The internationalisation of business activities by means of taking participations in consortium banks, which have grown rapidly in the last few years, is of lesser significance for American banks.

While Chase Manhattan Bank has participated in several co-operative international banks, the FNCB has so far not entered a relationship of this kind. The Bank of America has a share in the SFE Group (Société Financière Européenne, Paris/Luxembourg), the Bank of America Ltd., London, the Banque Ameribas S.A. Luxembourg and the European Brazilian Bank Ltd. (EUROBRAZ), London. The multinational commitment of the Chase Manhattan Bank includes its participation in the Orion Group in London. A table of the most important multinational consortium bank establishments in Appendix 1 reveals the presence of further American banks — mostly medium sized banks.

e) *Significance of foreign business for American banks*

The growing significance of foreign business for American banks is to be found notably in its function of complementing their domestic business. Thus in 1971 the share of foreign borrowers in the total credit extended by FNCB was 39 per cent, for the Morgan Guaranty 26 per cent, for the Bank of America 25 per cent and for the Chase Manhattan 22 per cent.[15] In 1971 the seven largest US banks [16] earned on average 28 per cent (22 per cent in the previous year) of their total earnings abroad.[17] In the lead was the FNCB with 42 per cent, after 38 per cent in 1970. International earnings continued to grow in the following years. A study by Salomon Brothers shows that for the top ten US banks international earnings accounted for 38.5 per cent of total earnings in 1973 and around 43.0 per cent in 1974.[18] The high

Table 6. US merchant banks in London

US merchant bank subsidiary	Year of establishment	Parent bank	Issued share capital (in millions)
First International Bancshares Ltd.	1973	First International Bancshares Inc.	US-$20
International Marine Banking Co.	1971	Marine Midland Bank	£ 5.084
Chase Manhattan Ltd.	1973	Chase Manhattan Bank NA	£ 4
Manufacturers Hanover Ltd.	1968	Manufacturers Hanover Trust (75%) N. M. Rothschild & Sons (10%) Riunione Adriatica di Sircurta (10%) Long Term Credit Bank of Japan (5%)	£ 1.25
Bank of America International Ltd.	1971	Bank of America International S.A., Luxembourg[a]	£ 5.0
Wells Fargo Ltd.	1972	Wells Fargo Bank	£ 2
Citicorp International Bank Ltd.	1973	First National City Corporation	£ 2
Continental Illinois Ltd.	1972	Continental Illinois Corp.	£ 1.75
Bankers Trust International Ltd.	1968	Bankers Trust Co.	£ 1.5
First Chicago Ltd.	1970	First National Bank of Chicago	£ 0.1
First National Boston Ltd.	1972	First National Bank of Boston	

Note
a. Bank of America International S.A. is owned by Bank of America, San Francisco (55%), Banque de Paris et des Pays-Bas (22.5%) and Kleinwort Benson (22.5%).

Source
Notebook Britain, US banks in London, in *The Banker,* Vol. 123, No. 567 (May 1973) p. 449 and "Eurocurrency Banks" in London, in *The Banker,* Vol. 124, No. 585 (November 1974) p. 1395.

share contributed by foreign earnings in 1971 can be attributed firstly to the increase in foreign lending and secondly to the fat profits earned on foreign exchange business during the upheavals in the international currency markets, while the increased earnings in 1974 reflect the marked improvement in spreads and the bias towards size.

Furthermore the close-knit nature of the US foreign branch networks — claims on each other tripled between September 1969 and June 1972 to $10 billions — highlights the considerable influence they can exert on international capital movements. By reason of their flexible business policy they can, in a short period of time, transfer very large funds from one financial market to another.[19]

Foreign business will clearly in future continue to play an important role for American banks. In the extension of their activities, regions that have been relatively insignificant in the total in the past — notably in the Middle East — will obviously gain in importance. Equally, it is possible that the volume of business of the European branches will show only a gradual rate of growth, if the suspension of the Interest Equalisation Tax and the other controls on capital exports lead eventually to a further transfer of the demand for capital from the European to the US markets.

3.2. British banks abroad

a) *The British banking system*

By reason of the significant position of Great Britain in world trade and its close economic links with the countries of the Commonwealth, British banks have long been represented in strength in foreign countries.[20]

Before this international presence is described, it appears necessary however to outline the characteristics of the British system in its original form and in its more recent development.[21]

The British banking system is notable for its historically strongly marked specialised character. Amongst the various banking sectors are to be found domestic or deposit banks, overseas banks, discount houses, merchant banks and saving institutions. The London clearing banks, as the largest group of deposit banks, have concentrated predominantly on short-term lending and deposit business as well as on the related money transmission mechanism. Overseas banks are banks which, whilst being represented in London, conduct most of their business outside Great Britain. This group consists of British institutions with foreign branches and foreign banks with branches in London. The discount houses fulfil a principal function on the money market by providing means for evening out short-term liquidity positions, above all amongst the deposit banks. In the group of merchant banks may be included both the accepting houses and the issuing houses. Accepting houses are mainly active in the field of foreign trade financing by acceptance credits while both they and the issuing houses conduct new issue business, financial advisory services for companies, the administration of portfolios for private and institutional investors as well as the introduction of foreign securities (bonds and shares) on the London stock exchange.

For some time there has been evidence of changes taking place in the structure of the British banking system.[22] As a result of greater competition — springing not least from the influx of foreign banks into London — the traditional demarcation lines have been increasingly abandoned, whilst at the same time the element of concentration has increased within as well as between individual financial institutions. The trend towards the development of "Universal", or all-purpose, banks is exemplified in the fact that the clearing banks grant medium and long-term export credits and occasionally long-term loans to finance capital investment and even to some extent carry out issuing business. Some merchant banks, for their part, have pushed strongly into the short-term commercial banking business of the clearing banks.[23] This restructuring of British banking is reflected also in the foreign business of British banks.

b) *Overseas representation of the clearing banks*

Before the 1960s the clearing banks maintained, alongside their world-wide correspondent bank networks, hardly any direct branches overseas, but were represented mainly by subsidiaries and affiliated banks. In the following years they stepped up their international involvement, often by taking participations in joint ventures and by extending their interests in the British overseas banks. These banks, which had begun the construction of worldwide branch networks more than 100 years ago, were integrated into the international strategy of the clearing banks and form a nucleus of their international representation (see Table 7).

The main regions in which the British overseas banks established themselves were the developing countries of today. Each of the banks concentrated on a particular country or a certain continent—Barclays, for instance, on Africa. In numerous countries these banks played a decisive part in the construction and development of the banking system. Their main functions are in the servicing and financing of foreign trade, arranging finance for investment purposes and giving financial advice. This regionally-orientated policy was successful, as long as British banks were the most significant foreign banking investors.[24] With the increase in the foreign investments of other banks in the 1960s, however, an expansion of their regionally specialised coverage became necessary. Other factors helping to speed up the adaptation of the British overseas banks to a more truly international orientation were the loosening of the Commonwealth as a trading area, the disintegration of the sterling currency block and the growth of political and financial risks in the developing countries, which led in some cases to the nationalisation of British banks overseas branches.[25]

In addition the clearing banks have, again mostly by way of their participation in British overseas banks, extended their commitment in continental Europe, in the United States and latterly also in the Pacific area.[26] Table 8 shows in which continental European countries the clearing banks are represented by branches, subsidiaries and representative offices.

Table 7. Participations held by other banks in the principal British overseas banks[a], 1974

British Overseas Banks	Participating Bank	Percentage Interest
Barclays Bank International Ltd.[b]	Barclays Bank	100 %
Lloyds & Bolsa International Bank Ltd.[c]	Lloyds Bank	55.4%
	Mellon National Bank and Trust Company	12.6%
Australia and New Zealand Banking Group	Barclays Bank Group	9.9%
Eastern Bank	Chartered Bank	100 %
National Bank of New Zealand Ltd.	Lloyds Bank Group	100 %
National and Grindlays Bank[d]	First National City Bank	40.0%
	Lloyds Bank[e]	
Standard and Chartered Banking Group	Chase Manhattan Bank	13.8%
	National Westminster Bank	9.2%
	Midland Bank	4.6%
Standard Bank of West Africa	Standard Bank	100 %
Westminster Foreign Bank[f]	National Westminster Bank	100 %

Notes

a. British overseas banks are those members of the British Overseas and Commonwealth Banks Association which are in British ownership and which have their head offices in London.

b. This bank is a subsidiary of Barclays Bank and developed out of Barclays Bank D.C.O. (Dominion, Colonial and Overseas), in which Barclays had a 54.95 per cent interest.

c. This bank was the result of the merger in 1971 of the Bank of London and South America (Bolsa) and Lloyds Bank Europe. Lloyds & Bolsa International Bank Ltd. became a wholly owned subsidiary of Lloyds Bank Ltd. in 1973. The name of this subsidiary was changed to Lloyds Bank International Ltd. in April 1974.

d. The name of National & Grindlays Bank was changed to Grindlays Bank on January 1, 1975.

e. Lloyds Bank Ltd. holds 41.4% of National and Grindlays Holdings Ltd. which owns 60% of National & Grindlays Bank.

f. Renamed International Westminster Bank on January 1, 1973.

Sources

Bank annual reports for 1974 and: The "big four" part company, in *The Banker,* Vol. 123, No. 570 (August 1973) p. 943.

Table 8.   The clearing banks in continental Europe, 1974

	Belgium	Germany	France	Italy	Netherlands	Switzerland	Spain
Barclays[a]	B	B	S,R	S	B	R,S	–
Lloyds[b]	S	B	B,S	–	B,S	B	B
Midland	R,P	R,P	P	P	P	R	–
National Westminster[c]	B	B,P	B	P	–	–	R

Legend
S = subsidiary
R = representative office
B = branch
P = partner bank

Notes
a. Including Barclays Bank International.
b. Including Lloyds Bank International.
c. Including Westminster Foreign Bank (from January 1, 1973 International Westminster Bank).

Sources
The "big four" part company, in *The Banker,* Vol. 123, No. 570 (August 1973) Table 2, p. 939; International Banking: How British strategics differ, in *The Banker,* Vol. 124, No. 582 (August 1974) p. 925.

Barclays Bank has been represented in France for 50 years through its subsidiary Barclays Bank S.A., which currently operates 22 branches there, and in Switzerland by its 51 per cent participation in the Société Bancaire Barclays (Suisse) S.A. as well as its branches. In Belgium, Netherlands and Italy it has been able to offer a full banking service only since 1972. While it opened a branch in Belgium, in Italy a 51 per cent stake was acquired in Banca Castellini, which is now called Banca Barclays Castellini S.p.A., and in Holland a 70 per cent interest was purchased in Bankhaus Kol & Co. (Barclays Kol & Co. N.V.). The bank's activity in Germany was stepped up further with the establishment of a second subsidiary. In addition, Lloyds Bank International Ltd. is represented on the continent with 40 branches and International Westminster Bank with a total of 10 branches.

In the face of the growing demand for capital from European and multinational enterprises and the increasing attraction of the EEC countries for British banks the clearing banks have also – with the exception of Lloyds – participated in multinational bank establishments. In 1972 Lloyds made just an informal arrangement with the Commerzbank and the Crédit Lyonnais to facilitate the extension of credits, on a mutual basis, in sterling or in Deutschemarks or francs to customers of the bank. The formation of Midland and International Banks Ltd. (MAIBL) in 1964 was the first multinational bank establishment.

In the United States, a further principal region for foreign investment, the clearing banks are again represented partly through the overseas banks, which were the first British banks to be established there with full branches.[27] Barclays has for a long time been represented by two branches in New York and in 1965 founded in California the Barclays Bank California, which maintains in the West 28 branches of the United States and one in Grand Cayman. The take over of the Long Island Trust Company with 29 branches planned for 1973 was not permitted by the US authorities, but Barclays was allowed later to take over a smaller bank, the First Westchester National Bank, which was renamed Barclays Bank of New York, with 25 offices. Lloyds is active in the United States through a branch of the Lloyds & Bolsa International Bank in New York, which measured by deposits is one of the largest foreign banks in the United States and is traditionally very strongly engaged in the field of trade financing between the United States, Great Britain and Latin America.[28] The reason why this bank's representation in the United States was limited in comparison with its representation in Europe and Latin America for some years was because of the fact that Mellon National Bank and Trust Company/USA held a participation in Lloyds & Bolsa International Bank.[29] But this link has now been severed, and Lloyds has bought a bank in California, called at that time First Western bank and Trust Co. and now part of the Lloyds group.

National Westminster committed itself in the United States by opening a branch only at the end of the 1960s, and the Midland Bank started by changing its representative office, existing since 1945, to an agency and then to a branch, the activities of which were transferred in stages to the European American Banking Corporation. This had been founded in 1968 by Midland together with three European Banks and, with its sister institution, European American bank and Trust Company, specialises in the financing of foreign trade — mainly with European countries — as well as offering a full banking service for American and European clients.[30] In 1974 it took over the Franklin National Bank after that bank had collapsed. A table of the most important subsidiaries and affiliated companies of the British clearing banks can be found in Appendix 3.

c) *Overseas representation of merchant banks and discount houses*

Apart from the clearing banks and British overseas banks, a number of merchant banks and discount houses are represented abroad. The merchant banks, which had been active since the 19th century, and before, in international finance, expanded rapidly in the 1960s.[31] This expansion was based primarily on the growth of the Euro-currency markets, where they played a very important part, and was strengthened by the deep involvement on the part of some banks in the international bond market.[32] The expansion of their activity abroad was accomplished in various ways. On the one hand the merchant banks intensified their traditional correspondent bank relationships and on the other hand they institutionalised a number of their international connections either by the launching of joint ventures with other foreign banks (cf. Appendix 1) or by the establishment of subsidiaries or the acquisition of stakes in foreign banks. Table 9 shows in which countries or regions the merchant banks have taken interests in foreign or international financial institutions. By reason of their flexible approach to business they are in a position to adjust the services they offer constantly to the demands of their large number of customers and to offer them a comprehensive banking service.[33]

Table 9. *Participations held by merchant banks in foreign financial institutions*

	foreign institutions					international institutions	
	USA	Canada	Europe	Australia	other countries	finance companies and banks	investment companies
Arbuthnot Latham					M		
Baring Brothers		P		P	P	P	
Wm. Brandt			P	M			
Brown Shipley			P				
Charterhouse		M,P			P	P	M,P
A. Gibbs	P	P		M,P	M		
Guiness Mahon			M		M		
Hambros	M		M,P	P	P	P	
Hill Samuel	M		M,P	M	M,P		
Kleinwort	M		M	P	P	P	M,P
Lazard		M	P	P		P	
Mercury Securities	M		M,P				
Montagu Trust		M	M,P	P	P	P	P
Morgan Grenfell		P	M	P	P	P	P
Rea Brothers			P				
N. M. Rothschild						P	P
Schroder	M		M,P	P	M,P		

Legend
M = Majority participation(s) or branch(es)
P = Participation(s)

Source
Sandra Mason: Merchant banking today and in future, in *Journal of Business Finance,* Vol. 3 (1971) No. 4, p. 12.

Within the discount houses group, the last few years have again witnessed a strong trend towards a diversification of their activities. However, only a few of the 11 discount houses (a number reduced by mergers) extended their activity by undertaking new commitments abroad (see Table 10).

Table 10. Participations held by discount houses in foreign institutions

Discount house	Participation	when acquired
Cater, Ryder & Co. Ltd.	Martin Corporation, Sydney	1966
	Peterson Beiley, New York	1968
	Marshall Dague Bie (Head office in Geneva, branches in Paris and London, representative office in Toronto since 1970)	1968
Alexander's Discount Company Ltd.	Westralian International, Australia	1970
Clive Discount Company Ltd.	B.B. Maxwell, Toronto, through Guy Butler	1969
Gillett Brothers Discount Company Ltd.	2 interests in South Africa	1959/60

Source
Simon Proctor: First moves to set up abroad, in *The Financial Times,* No. 25189 (July 1, 1970).

d) *Outlook*

British banks, which have together historically maintained a far-flung branch network abroad, will strengthen their foreign representation further in the next few years. In this process an increasing interest will be shown in continental Europe, where the banks will concentrate either on the establishment of branches and subsidiaries—the way favoured by Lloyds Bank and Barclays Bank—or on the acquisition of participations, the method to be employed perhaps by National Westminster Bank.

3.3. German banks abroad

The German banking system is distinguished by the predominance of the all-purpose bank, the business activities of which include not only accepting deposits and granting credits but also all types of securities business. The institutions under private law as well as those under

29

public law and the associated co-operative banking sector are all predominantly of the "universal" bank type. In addition to these, there are a number of special institutions – for instance mortgage banks, instalment credit institutions and so forth. In the last decade a strong "concentration" movement has taken place within the German banking system. While in the fields of the public sector banks and the private banks, this process frequently involved mergers, the large banks have been tidying up and extending their interests in domestic credit institutions, acquiring some majority holding and sorting out small holdings – partly by the exchange of appropriate participations between each other. The territorial expansion of the large banks in Germany has taken place – in contrast to experience abroad – predominantly *via* the construction of branches and agencies.

a) *Extent and form of foreign investment*

After the loss of foreign assets twice this century, German financial institutions were very hesitant to venture forth again. Up to the 1960s they concentrated on the construction and completion of a worldwide network of correspondent bank relationships and representatives for conducting their traditional foreign business. They established hardly any foreign establishments of their own. At the end of 1963 there were only three German bank branches abroad – two branches of the Deutsch-Asiatische Bank and a branch of the Deutsche Ueberseeische Bank.[34]

With the expansion of German trade and the increasing foreign direct investments undertaken by German industrial enterprises,[35] German financial institutions in the 1960s embarked upon larger foreign investments. The value of direct investments by German credit institutions increased from DM 103.8 millions to DM 1,779.9 millions between 1961 and 1973, equivalent to a yearly rate of increase of 26.7 per cent on average (see Table 11). The growth rate in the years 1967 to 1971 increased by 30.1 per cent on average. In the total of all German direct investments abroad the share of the credit institutions is small but growing; it was 2.7 per cent in 1961 and 5.5 per cent in 1973. The yearly average growth rates of their foreign

30

Table 11. Development of overseas direct investment by German financial institutions in comparison with total German direct investment, 1961-73

Year[a]	Value of direct investment by German financial institutions (DM millions)	Change on previous year (%)	Value of total German direct investment (DM millions)	Change on previous year (%)	Share of direct investment by financial institutions in the total (%)
1961	103.8	–	3,842.5	–	2.7
1965	206.3	98.7[b]	8,317.1	116.5[b]	2.5
1966	229.8	11.4	9,995.3	20.2	2.3
1967	314.3	36.8	12,056.8	20.6	2.6
1968	569.5	81.2	14,349.0	19.0	4.0
1969	691.2	21.4	17,618.3	22.8	3.9
1970	771.9	11.7	21,113.2	19.8	3.7
1971	928.0	20.2	23,780.7	12.6	3.9
1972	1,199.1	29.2	26,596.1	11.8	4.5
1973	1,779.9	48.4	32,235.0	21.2	5.5

Notes
a. At year-end.
b. Increase on 1961.

Source
Ministry of Economics and the author's calculations.

31

investments were during this period the fastest of any branch of the economy, before the chemical and automobile industries.[36]

Apart from the big banks, which are the main investors, regional banks, private banks and central giro institutions have engaged in international activity predominantly by taking participations and entering into joint ventures. Subsidiaries were established in great numbers in Luxembourg but out of 13 leading German credit institutions the number of foreign branches maintained by them was until very recently small (see Appendices 1 and 4).

b) *Main centres of foreign activities*

When one considers the regional distribution of the foreign representation of German banks, some banks are found to have concentrated on the developing countries, but the centre of gravity is located in Europe, above all in London and Luxembourg (see Appendices 1 and 4). As regards the vehicle for their international expansion, German banks chose predominantly the acquisition of interests in other companies. During the 1960s however the "joint venture" route, in which banks from various countries take a share in a consortium bank or other co-operative bank, gained increasing significance for German banks. In addition, their activities were widened through the establishment of subsidiary companies in Luxembourg and recently by the opening of branches in London.

(i) *Joint ventures in Europe*. German banks have shares in 29 of the most important consortium banks or other multibank ventures, most of which have their head offices in Europe (see Appendix 1). The leading German partners in these co-operative ventures are the Commerzbank, the Deutsche Bank, the Dresdner Bank and the Westdeutsche Landesbank Girozentrale. The foundation for their cross-frontier co-operation consist of the following bank groupings:

— European Bank Inter-   Deutsche Bank
  national Company (EBIC)
— Société Financière   Dresdner Bank
  Européenne (SFE)

32

— Associated Banks of Europe Corp. (ABECOR)	Dresdner Bank
— Orion	Westdeutsche Landes-bank Girozentrale
— EUROPARTNER	Commerzbank

The EBIC, ABECOR and EUROPARTNER groups are composed only of European banks, whereas the SFE and Orion groups, apart from European banks, also include banks from the United States, Canada and Japan. The ABECOR group takes in several of the European partners of the SFE. A special feature of this group, in contrast to the other groups, is that it includes two banks from one country — Dresdner bank and Bayerische Hypotheken- and Wechsel-Bank. Besides a continual exchange of information between the participating banks, the joint ventures undertake specialised activities some of which overlap with the services offered by the individual parent banks. They represent a relaxed kind of relationship for the partner banks in that, on the one hand there is the possibility of dissolving such a co-operative club without undue difficulty, and on the other hand the group can control the entry of further suitable partners. Thus the number of member banks of EBIC has increased since its establishment from 4 to 7; that of the SFE group has risen from 6 to 8 and of the Orion group from 4 to 6.

The co-operative arrangement between the Commerzbank, the Banco di Roma, the Crédit Lyonnais and the Banco Hispano-Americano differs from the other groups in so far as the banks co-operate directly with each other. They intend to co-operate closely in all fields of activity with the long-term aim of effecting a „quasi-merger". For international business this means the establishment and expansion of an integrated banking network — in third countries as well as in the countries of the banks involved — which should enable the banks to put at the disposal of their clients an integrated, comprehensive, range of services.

A number of joint ventures in Europe have specialised in medium and long-term credit business. By reason of the large expansion of the financing requirements of industrial enterprises, the increase in the

33

number of multinational enterprises and the gap between short- and long-term financial markets, this type of credit gained increasing importance.[37]

The most important consortium banks for this business are the following, established by the EBIC, SFE, Orion and Europartner groups:

— Banque Européenne de Crédit   EBIC
  (BEC)
— Banque de la Société Finan-   SFE
  cière Européenne (BSFE)
— Orion Termbank LTD.[38]   Orion
— International Commercial   EUROPARTNER
  Bank (ICB)

The international banks specialising in this field of business are notable for their high degree of flexibility.[39]

They can structure loans according to the purpose for which finance is required, and the amount, maturity, currency and interest rate, in a very flexible manner. In addition there is the possibility of making further changes during the life of the credit. The expansion of business in consequence of the huge size of the Euro-markets, especially in the field of medium-term credits, gradually led to a sharpening of competition and thereby to a decrease in profit margins on this business.[40] This situation also encouraged a tendency for banks to shoulder increased risks of bad debts.[41] Apart from the consortium banks' own capital, deposits and stand-by credits of the partner banks, the Euro-Market constitutes the most important funding source for them.[42]

Besides the establishment of these special institutions for medium and long-term credit business, banks have also founded other types of joint ventures aimed at improving the services they could offer. Some of these concentrated on investment and issuing business, others on leasing and real estate financing. The international leasing activities of the Orion group were for instance brought together in Orion

34

Leasing Holdings Ltd., London, and the Multinational Orion Leasing Holdings N.V., Amsterdam. It is intended to expand the network of leasing offices to 25 in 30 countries by 1976.[43] By developing the international concept of its leasing activities the Orion group is aiming especially to cater for the growing needs of multinational enterprises for this type of financing.

In addition the Westdeutsche Landesbank and its affiliated company, the Rheinisch-Westfälische Immobilien-Anlagegesellschaft, have recently been active internationally in the real estate sector. Together with finance companies from Great Britain, the Netherlands, Belgium and France it founded the multinational property company, European Property Investment Company, with a head office in the Netherlands.

A further development of the joint venture is towards a regional specialisation. For instance, with the participation of the Banco Espirito Santo de Commercial de Lisboa and the Swiss Bank Corporation, the Orion group founded the Libra Bank [44] in London, which specialises in providing loans and services for customers in South America. Also, the EBIC partners have, together with Arab banks, established three ventures in Europe, the European Arab Holding S.A., Luxembourg, the European Arab Bank, Brussels, and the European-Arab Bank GmbH, Frankfurt, to specialise in European-Arab business. Again, through SFE the Dresdner Bank holds a share in the Compagnie Arabe et Internationale d'Investissement (CAII) in Luxembourg—another company involved in the fast-growing field of Middle East consortium banking. Several of the consortium banks have also established representative offices and branches of their own in other regions.

Apart from the large banks there are also several private banks which have entered relations with other European banks in order to strengthen their international business; for example, Sal. Oppenheim jr. & Cie. participates in the Rothschild Intercontinental Bank Ltd., and M. M. Warburg-Brinckmann, Wirtz & Co. in S. G. Warburg & Co. International Holdings Ltd.

(ii) *Subsidiary companies and branches in Europe.* In the last 10 years, German credit institutions, apart from participating in other financial institutions, have also enlarged their activities by the establishment of subsidiaries in Luxembourg, as well as lately also branches in London (see Appendix 4). By reason of its liberal banking, foreign exchange and holding company legislation as well as its involvement in the Euro-markets Luxembourg has become for German banks a prime centre of interest.[45] Apart from the three large banks, nine more credit institutions are represented there with subsidiaries.

— Berliner Handels-Gesellschaft/Frankfurter Bank —
  Deutsche Genossenschaftskasse
— Bayerische Vereinsbank
— Bankhaus Georg Hauck und Sohn
— Deutsche Girozentrale — Deutsche Kommunalbank
— Bayerische Hypotheken- und Wechsel-Bank
— Vereinsbank in Hamburg
— Berenberg Bank Joh. Berenberg, Gossler & Co.
— M. M. Warburg-Brinckmann, Wirtz & Co.
— Westdeutsche Landesbank — Girozentrale

These subsidiaries are active mainly in international loan syndication as well as in Euro-currency dealing and Euro-bond trading. Their growing significance for German credit institutions is demonstrated by the rapid growth in their total assets. The total assets of the subsidiaries of just the three major bank subsidiaries increased from approximately DM 2 billions in 1970 to about DM 8.3 billions in 1972 and to DM 14.6 billions in 1974.

The strong growth of the Luxembourg subsidiaries, which took place despite the harsher application of the German cash deposit scheme, can be explained partly by the multinational composition of the banks' customers. It is also due partly, however, to a transfer of business as a deliberate policy decision. German banks channelled financial transactions increasingly through Luxembourg because their subsidiaries could fund themselves on the Euro-markets without becoming subject to minimum reserve requirements — in Luxembourg there are no such requirements.

36

Table 12. Business activity of the various Luxembourg subsidiaries of German banks

	End 1974	
	Total assets (DM billions)	Capital (DM millions)
Compagnie Financière de la Deutsche Bank AG[a]	5.8	60
Compagnie Luxembourgeoise de Banque S.A. (CLB)[b]	4.8	100
Commerzbank International S.A.	4.0	53
Westdeutsche Landesbank International S.A.[a]	2.7	80

Notes
a. Year ending 30 Sept. 1974.
b. Year ending 31 March 1974.

Source
Bank annual reports, 1974.

Recently a few German banks have also opened branches in London. The first was the Dresdner Bank, which opened a branch at the beginning of 1973 and this was followed in second place by the Westdeutsche Landesbank-Girozentrale and in the third place by the Commerzbank. These were followed by Investitions- und Handels-Bank and Bank für Gemeinwirtschaft. By contrast the Deutsche Bank is represented by a representative office, which however may possibly be changed to a branch at a later date.

(iii) *Presence in the United States.* In the United States German banks are represented by companies founded by their "European joint-venture clubs" and also by branches. The EBIC institutions (Deutsche Bank), "European-American Banking Corporation" and "European-American Bank and Trust Company", form the largest European banking group in New York. In 1972 a branch was established in Los Angeles, and in 1974 this group took over the Franklin National Bank after that bank had collapsed. These companies constitute the most important joint ventures of the EBIC group. The Deutsche Bank, with the Schweizerische Bankgesellschaft, also operates in New York a joint subsidiary engaged in American securities business, the UBS-DB Corporation.[46]

Turning to the ABECOR group, (Dresdner Bank, Bayerische Hypotheken-und Wechsel-Bank) the broker-dealer affiliate is called the A.B.D. Securities Corporation and was opened in New York in 1972. To it was transferred the business of the German-American Securities Corporation, Boston, which had been founded by the Dresdner Bank in 1969, and the A.B.N. Corporation, New York, a subsidiary of ABECOR partner Algemene Bank Nederland. A.B.D. Securities Corporation carried out securities transactions in North America and maintains a branch in Boston. Further, the Dresdner Bank upgraded its New York and Los Angeles representative offices to branches in 1972 and 1974. The bank is also represented by a branch in Chicago (opened in 1974). The Commerzbank manages, together with both its "Europartners", an investment bank in New York called Europartners Securities, which is involved in securities brokerage and in American and international issuing business.[47] It maintains in addition, a branch in New York, which does export financing and commercial banking notably for subsidiaries of German corporations. The Westdeutsche Landesbank-Girozentrale is represented in New York by a representative office, which will be changed to a branch in the autumn of 1975, and through the New York representative office of Orion Bank, which was established in 1974.

(iv) *Presence in the Far East.* The financial centres of Tokyo, Singapore and Hong Kong have lately been of increasing interest to German banks. Commerzbank, together with Crédit Lyonnais and Banco di Roma, supports joint representative offices in Tokyo and Singapore. The Dresdner Bank is represented in Singapore by a branch and has a stake in the Asian and European Bank Ltd. (ASEAMBANK). In Tokyo it has applied for permission to open a branch. The Deutsche Bank is represented in Tokyo by the branch of the Deutsche Überseeische Bank. For the further extension of its activities it has, together with its EBIC partners, launched the

European-Asian Bank, which was developed out of the former Deutsch Asiatische Bank. This bank is active in the Asiatic area through five branches in Djakarta, Hong Kong, Karachi, Kuala Lumpur and Singapore.[48] The Westdeutsche Landesbank is represented in the Far East by the merchant bank Orion Pacific Ltd., established in 1974. In addition, a number of German banks have interests in finance companies in Australia.

(v) *Presence in underdeveloped countries.* German banks' investment in developing countries is relatively small. Stakes held in financial institutions in these countries often serve the continuing need to handle and finance trade with Germany whilst also helping to stimulate the development of an effective domestic banking system in these countries. Of special significance are the participations held in development banks and in financing institutions responsible for planning and carrying out smaller and medium-sized investments.[49] In Central and South America the Dresdner Bank and the Deutsche Bank both have footholds through the branches, participations and representative offices maintained by their subsidiaries, the Deutsch-Südamerikanische Bank and the Deutsche Ueberseeische Bank. For example almost one third of the total assets of the Deutsche Ueberseeische Bank is contributed by its foreign branches.[50] The predominant portion of the advances granted by both subsidiary companies serves the financing of international business, especially trade financing.[51]

In the developing countries of Africa and Asia the representation of German banks is effected through participations in local financial institutions, to an even greater extent than in Latin America.[52]

c) *The trend towards multinational banks*

The internationalisation of German banking will certainly be taken further in the next few years; for the demand from multinational industrial enterprises for international financing of their investments can be met only by international banks. German banks will on the one hand intensify their international co-operative relationships and, on the other, expand further their own branch networks in the world's international financial centres. They will also, as appropriate, establish more subsidiaries and acquire further participations in other companies abroad.

3.4. French banks abroad

a) *The French banking system*

The French banking system is characterised by a high degree of state regulation. A specialisation of the banks into three groups with a pre-ordained business structure was laid down by a law of 1945.[53] According to this, the following groups were differentiated: deposit banks (banques de dépots), were only allowed to accept deposits for terms of less than two years; business banks (banques d'affaires), which were also confined in their deposit-taking activities to short-term deposits; and banks for medium and long-term credit, which were not allowed to accept deposits with a period of time of less than two years.[54]

The big nationalised banks are considered to rank as deposit banks: these are the Banque Nationale de Paris (BNP) which emerged in 1966 from the merger of the two state institutions, the Banque Nationale pour le Commerce et l'Industrie (BNCI) and the Comptoir National d'Escompte de Paris (CNEP); the Crédit Lyonnais; and the Société Générale.[55]

However, in order to make the banks participate to a greater extent in the financing of industrial investment and also to intensify inter-bank competition several reforms were carried out between 1966 and 1969 which made the former structure of French banking of little significance.[56] Indeed, the differences between deposit banks and business banks hardly exist any longer. Both groups are developing in the direction of all-purpose banks. With the widespread suspension of official control over interest rates the banks allow on deposits and charge on loans, competition increased sharply amongst financial institutions and a move to greater concentration in the banking system was encouraged. This liberalisation has also contributed greatly to stimulating the international activities of French banks, which had been to some extent committed abroad for more than a century.[57]

The banks have extended their representation abroad mainly through setting up branches and subsidiaries, and also partly by the establishment of representative offices and the acquisition of stakes in other banks. In the 1960s they also became more interested in entering into co-operation with foreign banks in the form of joint ventures and, to a lesser extent, in the form of a cross-frontier integration of the partners' businesses.

Apart from the three big nationalised banks, the following French groups, in particular, are represented strongly abroad: the Compagnie Financiere de Suez, a most important French holding company which is represented abroad largely through the Banque de Suez et de l'Union des Mines (100 per cent owned), the Crédit Industrial et Commercial (70 per cent) and the Banque de l'Indochine (over 50 per cent); [58] and the far-flung group gathered round the holding company Compagnie Financière de Paris et des Pays-Bas, which owns the Banque de Paris et des Pays-Bas (100 per cent), Paribas International (100 per cent), the Union Bancaire (75 per cent)—founded as a holding company in 1971 to hold an 84 per cent stake in the Banque de l'Union Parisienne and a 31 per cent stake in the Crédit du Nord and Omnium de Participations Bancaires (OPB-PARIBAS), of which 27.34 per cent is held by the Cie. Financière and 46.68 per cent by the Banque de Paris et des Pays-Bas itself.

b) *Regional distribution of foreign representation*

As regards the regional distribution of their foreign representation, French banks are deeply entrenched in Europe, in Africa and in the Near and Middle East, with further big interest in Central, South, and North America (see Appendix 5).

In *Europe* the branches are the dominant form of representation. Of the total of about 50 branches, 30 are maintained by the Crédit

Lyonnais and 9 by the Banque de Paris et des Pays-Bas. While the representation of the Crédit Lyonnais is formed almost exclusively by branches, the other French banks are active to a larger extent also through subsidiaries. By reason of the close economic relations between France and Belgium as well as long-standing relations with Belgian banks, French banks are especially strongly represented in that country.[59]

French banks also followed the international trend towards a growing cross-frontier co-operation with foreign banks. The most important international links were formed by the Banque Nationale de Paris (BSFE/SFE), the Société Générale (EBIC group) and the Crédit Lyonnais – in the link-up with Banco di Roma, Commerzbank, and Banco Hispano Americano (see Appendix 1). These offered the French banks the possibility of expanding their international connections and of stepping up their activity on European markets in their efforts to satisfy the requirements of French and multinational corporations.

Examples of international co-operation cemented by an exchange of shares are the connection established between Banque Neuflize, Schlumberger, Mallet and the Dutch bank, Bank Mees & Hope, and that between Paribas and S. G. Warburg, London.[60] Paribas has acquired 25 per cent of S. G. Warburg, while Warburg has an indirect share, through a jointly-established subsidiary, in the Paribas banks in France, Belgium, the Netherlands and Switzerland.[61] Through this connection Paribas strengthened its position not only in London, but also in New York, where a joint subsidiary is to be established.

In North America French banks have really taken the plunge only in the last few years. Apart from eight representative offices and a branch of the Crédit Lyonnais, there is a subsidiary jointly owned by the Banque de Paris et des Pays-Bas, the Banque Nationale de Paris, and the Banque de l'Union Parisienne; in addition, in 1971 the BNP took over the entire capital of the French American banking Corporation, in which it had previously had a share of one third together with the Compagnie Financière de Suez and the Banque de l'Indochine (also each with one third share).[62] The agency maintained in San Francisco by the French American Banking Corp. was changed into a subsidiary, the French Bank of California, which conducts the full range of banking operations, and recently opened a branch in Los Angeles.[63]

Among the three big nationalised banks, the BNP has the strongest position in the United States. However, through its membership of the EBIC group, the Société Générale is active via their joint ventures — the European-American banking Corporation and European American Bank & Trust Company.

French banks are especially well entrenched in the former French colonial areas of Africa. As can be seen from Appendix 5 they are represented in this region through subsidiaries and associated banks and by the branches of these banks as well as to some extent through their own branches. Here the Crédit Lyonnais and the Banque Nationale de Paris are the most deeply committed banks. In Asia, the BNP, the Banque de l'Indochine and the Société Générale are predominant; in addition, the Banque de l'Indochine maintains three subsidiaries. In Central and South America, the French banks are represented by 19 branches (13 of Sudaméris, in which the Banque de l'Indochine and the Banque de Paris et des Pays-Bas participate, and 6 of BNP) as well as a number of subsidiaries which are active there, partly through extensive branch networks of their own.

c) *Stronger co-operation*

The far-flung branch networks of the French banks are not likely to be extended further in the colonial areas. Further expansion abroad will take the shape mainly of a deepening of their co-operative relationships with European banks.

3.5. Japanese banks abroad

a) *Changes in the Japanese banking system* [64]

The banking system in Japan is characterised by a high degree of specialisation. Amongst the important banking groups, besides foreign exchange banks, both long-term credit banks and the trust banks have to be distinguished. The deposit banks have a local character—with the notable exception of the so-called City banks. The City banks are the largest and most important banks in Japan. They account for more than 30 per cent of the deposits at all Japanese financial institutions. They are engaged mainly in short and medium-term lending for large enterprises. The scope of the operations of the long-term credit banks extends in particular to industrial financing. In their refinancing operations these banks can, however, unlike the deposit banks, accept only medium-term deposits. The trust banks function mainly as trust companies for pension and investment funds.

Up to the 1960s the Japanese banks focused their activities mainly on the domestic market. Their international expansion is a recent phenomenon, connected closely with the development of Japan's overall foreign economic policy. During the period of reconstruction of the Japanese economy after the Second World War the opportunities for carrying out international business were very limited for Japanese banks. For many years the Bank of Tokyo was given a prior ranking position.[65]

As the successor of the officially authorised foreign exchange bank of Japan before the war, the Yokohama Specie Bank, it remains the only bank specialised in foreign exchange as well as in export and import financing. It is not subject to control in its conduct of international banking or as regards the establishment of branches abroad.[66] Only very hesitantly did the Japanese Ministry of Finance give other banks permission to open branches abroad. The first was the Bank of Tokyo in 1952; and in the same year four other banks received permission to open six branches.[67]

With the improvement of the Japanese balance of payments in the second half of the 1960s measures were introduced for the liberalisation of trade and capital transactions. Against the background of increasing export surpluses and the necessity for securing long-term raw material supplies, Japanese industrial enterprises extended their activity abroad considerably through direct investments. Although the net value of Japanese overseas direct investments is still a long way behind that of other industrial countries, the average annual growth rate in 1965-70 was more rapid than that of any other country.[68]

This trend towards internationalisation has evidently also contributed to the re-orientation of the Japanese banking system. The strict controls and restrictions on the foreign business of the banks were relaxed. The Ministry of Finance became more liberal in allowing the establishment of branches abroad and the carrying out of other foreign activities, and in autumn 1970 abolished completely the restrictions on the granting of credits by foreign branches.

b) *Extent and form of foreign activities*

Today Japanese banks have footholds in almost all the larger financial centres of the main industrial countries and of developing countries. At the end of 1974 16 Japanese banks were represented abroad as against 12 institutions in 1966. The number of branches in the meantime increased, between 1966 and 1974, from 58 to 106, while the number of representative offices shot ahead from 24 to 81 (see Table 13). The focus of the banks' international activities has, however, shifted in recent years to the establishment of subsidiaries abroad and to the taking of participations in multinational financial institutions; the number of these participations reached 70 at end-1972 and by 1974 increased to 190 (see Table 13).

The last few years have witnessed a marked diversification of the business activities of Japanese banks abroad, but the main tasks in the short term remain as always financing the trade of Japanese enterprises, the provision of financial resources for this trade and the conduct of foreign exchange business arising out of trade transaction.[69] The financial resources are provided primarily by way of acceptance credits at US banks and Euro-dollar credits. So Japanese banks in New York count as the largest source of demand for acceptance credits.[70] The business is carried out by branches and foreign subsidiaries, or local companies in which an interest is held.

Table 13. Japanese banks abroad

	Foreign branches				Representative offices				Participations			
	1966	1972	1973	1974	1966	1972	1973	1974	1966	1972	1973	1974
North America	17	26	27	32	7	15	16	16	6	10	14	21
Latin America	6	9	10	10	–	3	8	10	4	12	21	26
Europe	16	25	30	33	6	15	14	11	–	28	44	56
Africa (including Near East)	–	–	–	–	4	3	3	10	–	–	–	4
Far East (including Australia and New Zealand)	19	30	30	31	7	27	35	34	3	20	65	83
Total	58	90	97	106	24	63	76	81	13	70	144	190

Sources
Ichiro Takeuchi: Japanese banks overseas, in *The Banker's Magazine*, Vol. 204 (1967) No. 1483, p. 175. Expansion of Japanese banking abroad, in *Euromoney:* Japan – the rising force in international banking (March 1973) p. 7; Japanese banks overseas in 1973, in *Euromoney:* International banking in Japan – a survey (March 1974) p. 9; Japanese banks overseas in 1974, in *Euromoney* (April 1975) pp. 63.

But with the increasing demand for medium and long-term credits for the financing of direct investments by Japanese industrial companies abroad, the interest of the banks in longer-term foreign business has also grown rapidly. Beyond this they are striving to extend their activities further by taking participations in international financial projects. On the one hand this new development led to the establishment of three investment banks, in which several Japanese banks participated. On the other hand a number of participations were acquired in existing multinational banks.

c) *Regional distribution of foreign activities*

A regional analysis shows that the Japanese banks have concentrated on the United States and Europe:[71] there are 16 banks with direct foreign representation and 2 representative offices in New York.

Another region of the United States of prime importance to them is California: 8 Japanese banks operate branches in Los Angeles and 3 in San Francisco. In addition, many subsidiaries or affiliated companies of Japanese banks are to be found in the United States. These play an extremely important role in that they can, by contrast to most branches, carry out all banking business, including investment business. The first subsidiary to be set up was the Bank of Tokyo Trust Company, founded in New York in 1955. The Bank of Tokyo has a 75.10 per cent share in the capital of $16.279 millions, and the Industrial Bank of Japan one of 24.90 per cent.[72] This company, established under American law, carried out all normal bank business and extended its field of business in 1971 with the establishment of a branch in London. In California, subsidiaries of the Bank of Tokyo and the Sumitomo Bank have been established for 20 years and maintain big networks of offices. At the beginning of 1972 the Mitsubishi Bank and the Sanwa Bank also established subsidiaries in California. In Chicago both the Bank of Tokyo and the Dai-Ichi Kangyo Bank are represented by subsidiaries, the Sanwa Bank and the Sumitomo Bank by branch offices, and four other banks by representative offices.

Collaboration between Japanese and American enterprises has been deepened by the formation of joint subsidiaries. For instance, Fuji Bank and First National City Bank founded in the middle of 1972 the Asia Pacific Capital Corp., with a capital of $6 millions, with the FNCB taking a 70 per cent share and the Fuji 30 per cent.[73] This company has its head office in the Bahamas, while the business catchment area is Hong Kong and Singapore. Moreover the Fuji Bank acquired in 1972 20,000 shares in the capital of FNCB, while the FNCB took a 10 per cent share in the capital of the Fuji National City Leasing Consulting Co. Ltd., and other stakes in the Fuyo General Lease Co. Ltd.[74]

The activities of Japanese banks in Europe concentrate on Great Britain and West Germany. Above all London, as an international financial centre and centre of the Euro-dollar market, has a great attraction for the Japanese. The Japanese banks have established 16 branches in the City of London. In Germany eight Japanese banks are represented through ten branches and a further five banks have representative offices.

In addition, three Japanese investment banks have been established in Europe. As early as 1968 the Bank of Tokyo established, in Paris, the Banque Européenne de Tokyo S.A. (BET) as a subsidiary with an initial capital of Ffr. 25 millions. In 1970 three other large banks took a share in this institution (Kyowa Bank, Bank of Kobe and Saitama Bank) as well as three long-term credit banks (Industrial Bank of Japan, Long-Term Credit Bank of Japan and Nippon Fudosan Bank). The second investment bank—Associated Japanese Bank (International) Ltd.—linked together four large banks (Sanwa Bank, Mitsui Bank, Dai-Ichi Bank and Kangyo Bank, the last two having since merged to form the Dai-Ichi Kangyo Bank) and the securities investment company Nomura Securities Co. The company, domiciled in London, with a capital of £ 3.5 millions, is owned by four partners with 25 per cent each. A third joint investment or consortia bank was founded at the end of 1970—the Japan International Bank — also in London. The shareholding partners are four large banks (Fuji, Sumitomo, Mitsubishi and Tokai) and three securities investment houses (Nikko, Daiwa and Yamaichi). The three investment banks finance themselves on the Euro-markets and

48

arrange mainly medium and long-term credits for subsidiaries of Japanese enterprises. Moreover they participate in international lending syndicates. An outstanding characteristic of these three institutions is that they were established by Japanese banks and security investment companies alone, in contrast to the usual multinational participation concept of such international consortia. This national approach is largely attributable to the restrictive policy of the Japanese Ministry of Finance, which until recently did not permit Japanese banks to participate in existing multinational banks.[75] Examples of the participation of Japanese banks in multinational joint enterprises are those of the Mitsubishi Bank in the Orion group in London, the Sumitomo Bank in the Société Financière Européenne (SFE) in Paris, the Industrial Bank of Japan in Rothschild Intercontinental, the Long Term Credit Bank in Manufacturers Hanover Ltd., in London, and the Tokai Bank in the Interunion-Banque in Paris (see Appendices 1 and 6).

The strong position of Japan in the trading patterns of other Asian countries as well as the growing significance of Singapore as the centre of the Asian-dollar market has led to a fast expansion of Japanese banks in Asia. In both Hong Kong and Singapore 14 Japanese banks maintain branches or representative offices.

The Asian-dollar market developed in Singapore at the end of the 1960s after the example set by the Euro-dollar market as the international money market, trading is mainly in dollars, but other currencies are dealt in.[76] The liberal supervision of capital imports by the Ministry of Finance in Singapore as well as the favourable geographical position of the Republic vis-à-vis other trade centres in the Far East, as for example Tokyo, Hong Kong and Sidney, have made possible this development. If this market cannot compete in terms of volume or the number of market participants with the Euro-market, its rapid growth points to its increasing importance as a money market and source of finance in Asia.

Australia has developed into a further important area for Japanese banks by reason of its close economic connections with Japan.

As Japanese credit institutions are not allowed to establish branches in Australia, they have involved themselves with other banks through the acquisition of participations in Australian finance companies, or through the establishment of joint enterprises. The first of these was in 1969, when the Bank of Tokyo founded Partnership Pacific Ltd., in Sydney, together with the Bank of America and the Bank of New South Wales. The capital of $6 millions is held equally by the three partners.[77] The activity of this company ranges from the granting of medium and long-term credits to the financing of projects (predominantly in primary industry) and the acquisition of equity stakes. Since then seven other Japanese banks have also taken stakes in Australian finance companies (see Appendix 6).

In addition, during 1974 Japanese banks expanded their activities in the Middle East. The number of representative offices increased to ten and the number of participations in local banks and investment companies reached four.[78]

d) *The trend towards participations*

In future Japanese banks will be deeply involved in international banking, because of the huge demand for capital by Japanese industrial concerns. The most popular route for expanding their presence abroad is likely to remain that of participations in foreign banks and finance houses. The pace of expansion of the banks could, however, slow down, if new restrictions were to be imposed on the overseas activities of Japanese banks in reaction to the changing foreign economic situation of Japan.

50

4

SIGNIFICANT FINANCIAL CENTRES
FOR BANKS

4.1. European centres

Examination of the foreign activity of Japanese and European banks has shown that only since the second half of the 1960s have foreign investments been made by banks to any large extent. As far as investment locations are concerned, Europe and the United States remain the most popular, joined recently by Far East and Middle East. The banks have concentrated mainly on the leading international financial centres. These centres stand out as offering comprehensive financing and investment possibilities through efficient institutions with top-level international business connections, i.e. they can efficiently carry out money and capital export and import transactions.[79]

Their ability to function in this way is, however, secured only by liberal economic and currency policies as well as liberal legislation.[80] The following chapter discusses several of the financial centres of Europe, New York and some of the financial centres of the Far East.

a) *London*

London, the oldest European financial centre, was able to develop again, in the 1960s, despite the never-ending economic and currency crises of Great Britain and the fast-diminishing significance of the sterling as a reserve and trading currency, into a leading international financial centre. Several factors contributed to this astonishing conjuring trick. On the one hand the pre-conditions for carrying out international business were fully satisfied through a rich variety of highly-developed specialised money and capital markets, insurance services, freight/transportation and shipping services.[81] Apart from this "infrastructure" of the City of London, it was above all the strong growth of the Euro-markets, and especially of the Euro-dollar market, that exercised such a strong attraction for many foreign banks and thereby increased decisively the significance of London as an international financial centre.[82] This development was considerably favoured by liberal regulations on branching and the absence of petty restrictions on the markets.[83] For instance, there are no minimum reserve requirements or interest-rate controls on Euro-currency business in London.

As the centre of the Euro-money market London plays a vital part. Almost 80 per cent of all transactions, of which more than two thirds are in Euro-dollars, are effected by branches of foreign banks in London. The number of banks represented by branches, subsidiaries or representative offices in London rose to 202 at the end of 1972.[84] This number was double that at the end of 1967. In the front rank were 50 American banks, followed by 19 Japanese and then the Italians and Swiss with 12 each. Apart from the 202 banks from 53 countries with their own direct representation, a further 43 foreign banks were represented by a participation in a multinational bank in London.[85]

The significance of the foreign banks in London is shown not only in their constantly increasing number but also in their strongly expanding volume of business, at least until the summer of 1974. Their total deposits increased from £ 4,955 millions at the end of 1967 to £ 12,508 millions at the end of 1969 and to £ 25,429 millions at end 1972.[86] Of this, the giant's share fell to American banks: in 1967 about 66 per cent, in 1969 about 78 per cent, and in 1972 about 69 per cent. Liabilities as well as assets are denominated predominantly in foreign currencies and are on behalf of foreign clients. The total credit extended to foreign residents increased between 1967 and 1972 from £ 3,038 millions to £ 14,972 millions, while the amount granted to residents rose in the same period from £ 545 millions to £ 2,095 millions.[87]

As regards loans to residents, the share of foreign currency credits extended by foreign banks increased from about 25 per cent at end 1967 to about 33 per cent at end 1969 and to about 38 per cent at end 1972, when it exceeded in terms of value the credit granted by the deposit banks and accepting houses in foreign currency.[88]

In the long-term area too London is one of the leading centres; despite the fact that such long-term financing by banks is a recent development there. This is evidenced not only in the market for medium-term credits, where the jointly-owned institutions of banks from various countries are particularly active, but also in the growth of Euro-bond issues.[89] The value of new Euro-bond issues with a maturity of 5 years and more increased between 1969 and 1971 from $ 2,993.7 millions to $ 3,755.7 millions.[90] Most loans are denominated as before in dollars (about 60 per cent by value), with Deutschemark issues accounting for about 25 per cent.[91]

The Euro-capital market has been intensively exploited by American corporations. Amongst investors in it, the most important groups come from continental Europe and the Middle East, the latter investing mostly through Swiss banks.

b) *Switzerland*

Next to London, Switzerland is counted as one of the international financial centres with the longest traditions. The development of Switzerland as a financial centre was encouraged by the marked international orientation of the banks, insurance companies and numerous holding companies there. Plainly, the significance of Switzerland's role lies also in its magnetism for foreign capital resulting from the thorough-going liberal economic and currency policy of the country, its tradition of the banking secrecy and its political neutrality. These factors justify the confidence of investors, and so promote Switzerland's status as a financial centre.[92]

A large part of the foreign money is re-invested abroad through the Swiss banking system. The cosmopolitan character of Switzerland as a financial entrepôt centre is highlighted by the large share of foreign business in the total business of the banks — amounting to 46 per cent of assets and 48 per cent of liabilities, in 1971.[93] The foreign assets of the Swiss banks active abroad amounted at the end of 1971 to Sfr. 97.3 billions, of which Sfr.36.0 billions was represented by trust business.[94] The foreign banks established in Switzerland had a share of 26 per cent, putting them in second place after the large banks, the share of which amounted to 65 per cent.[95] At the end of 1971 there were 98 foreign banks in Switzerland, including banks founded under Swiss law in foreign ownership and 13 subsidiaries of foreign banks.[96] They had a balance-sheet total of Sfr. 25,5 billions which corresponds to a share of 11 per cent in the total assets of all Swiss banks.[97]

The regulations on foreign banks have been, it is true, interpreted liberally, but according to Swiss banking legislation banks must maintain a relatively high ratio of own capital to liabilities. The demand for the strict observance of such ratio is seen as a reason for the relatively low share gained by foreign banks in Switzerland, in comparison with London.[98]

In domestic banking, foreign banks hardly make any mark; for the most part they possess only a small number of customers.[99] Plainly the main area of their business activity lies in foreign currency, trade and securities dealing.[100] The centre for this business is Zürich, which also dominates the gold trade; more than one third of gold sales are now made through Zürich.[101]

By reason of its financial weight, Switzerland represents one of the most important sources of funds in Europe. The close connections between the Swiss financial markets and foreign markets — especially the Euro-markets — has, intriguingly, been strengthened by the lack of an efficient money market in Switzerland itself. In contrast to other financial centres, in Switzerland only the capital market is of international importance. For many years it was the leading centre for the issue of foreign loans. With revival and the broader development of the European new issue market in the 1960s and the growing placing power of other centres, Germany for example, the significance of Switzerland in this field declined. Already in 1968 the total volume of Euro-bond loans, at $ 3.4 billions, exceeded by $ 0.4 billions the total volume of negotiable foreign loans.[102] The relative reduction in the total issue in Swiss francs was due mainly to the Swiss stamp duty as well as to the reluctance of the Swiss National Bank to see the Swiss franc used as an international issue currency.[103] The stamp duty is also the main reason why Swiss banks do not appear as managers or co-managers of Euro-bonds. They are, however, by reason of their huge "placing power", in a position to take between a third and half of all issues of Euro-bond securities, for placing with their clients.[104]

c) *Germany*

Until recently Germany was known as one of the most liberal capital markets in Europe, after Switzerland. With the adoption of full convertibility of the Deutschemark and the complete liberalisation of capital movements, the preconditions for the development of the German capital market to a true international market were fulfilled. This led first of all to large-scale foreign investments in Germany, and outward investment from Germany gathered momentum only in the second half of the 1960s. Apart from direct investments of German enterprises and the granting of foreign credits, the purchase of foreign loans—especially foreign DM loans—played an important part in this development. With the increase in Euro-bond issues, international loans denominated in Deutschemarks totalled $1,040.5 millions in 1969 and $ 859.8 millions in 1971.[105] Thus the Deutschemark became the second most important international loan currency after the dollar.[106]

Germany's significance as a trading and industrial nation, the development of the Deutschemark, as an international trading and loan currency, and, at least until recently, the freedom of its capital markets have all been powerful attractions for foreign banks. By reason of the decentralisation of the German banking system, several financial centres emerged: namely Düsseldorf, Frankfurt, Hamburg and Munich. Among these Frankfurt now has a dominating position – particularly as regards the number of foreign banks. For on the one hand Frankfurt is the main centre for the large banks and the seat of the Bundesbank, which intervenes on the foreign exchange market there, while on the other hand the Frankfurt stock exchange is, as measured by turnover, the largest in Germany. Furthermore Frankfurt's significance as an international securities and issuing centre has increased continuously in the last few years.

Foreign banks are represented in Germany mainly by branches. Subsidiaries and participations in German credit institutions have so far not been so important.[107] Subsidiaries of foreign banks are treated, according to the law governing the credit system, just in the same way as domestic credit institutions.[108]

The number of foreign banks with branches in Germany increased from 13 at the end of 1960 to 22 at end 1968, 29 at end 1971 and to 42 at end August 1973.[109] The 42 banks were represented by a total of 72 branches.[110] American banks, of which there are 13 with 30 branches, are most strongly represented. In second place are six Japanese banks with eight branches, followed by four French with ten branches and five British banks with six branches. Moreover there are about 100 representative offices of foreign banks and 30 banks established under German law predominantly in foreign ownership.

With the growing number of foreign branches, their volume of business has increased considerably. Their balance-sheet total increased from DM 1.0 billion at the end of 1960 to DM 6.8 billions at end 1968, DM 15.4 billions at the end of 1971 and DM 21.3 billions in June 1973.[111] If one compares the balance-sheet total of the foreign establishments with that of all domestic credit institutions their share in the last few years was 0.4 per cent in 1960, 1.0 per cent in 1968, 1.7 per cent in 1971 and 2.0 per cent in June 1973. American banks dominate here too. They account for more than two thirds of the balance-sheet totals of foreign branches. The 30 foreign-owned banks had comparatively small assets, reaching DM 4.3 billions at end 1971 and DM 5.9 billions at end 1972, which corresponds to a share of 0.4 per cent and 0.6 per cent in the total assets of all credit institutions.

The balance-sheet structure of foreign banks differs considerably from all other credit institutions.[112] On the assets side, claims on other credit institutions hold a dominating position. Their share in total assets increased from 60 per cent at the end of 1968 to 64 per cent at the end of 1971, with the largest share, of 34 per cent, being in claims on foreign banks, predominantly the parent banks (31 per cent). Credit extended to domestic non-banks increased during the same period from DM 2.0 to 4.7 billions while its share in their total assets rose only from 29 per cent to 31 per cent. A large part of the credits were granted to German subsidiaries of foreign companies. Credit extended to enterprises abroad, however, is small.

The main sources of funds for foreign branches in Germany are foreign banks, whose share in the balance-sheet total rose from 33 per cent at end 1968 to 58 per cent at end 1971. In total at the end of 1971 80 per cent of all liabilities was attributable to liabilities to credit institutions. On both sides of the balance-sheet relations with parent banks predominated. However, the small excess of balance and liabilities owed to parent banks over claims on them shows that the branches of foreign banks funded their local German business only to a small extent through their parent banks. The decreasing importance of domestic credit institutions as sources of finance for the foreign banks is shown in the decreased share they hold in the liabilities of foreign banks—one of 41 per cent in 1968 and 22 per cent in 1971. Deposits from non-banks, which dominate the business of domestic credit institutions, are insignificant for foreign bank branches, accounting for only 7 per cent of liabilities.

d) *Luxembourg*

In the last decade Luxembourg has grown in stature as an international financial centre. Its main attraction to foreign banks and finance companies lies in its liberal holding company, foreign currency and banking legislation as well as in its active foreign currency market.[113]

Holding companies are freed from taxes and other imposts, apart from the payment of a small tax at the time of establishment and a yearly tax of 0.16 per cent of the effective capital value.[114] These advantages have resulted in the establishments of numerous holding companies in Luxembourg. Their number is estimated at between 1,600 and 2,600.[115] According to the holding company legislation the following types are distinguished: group holding companies, financial holding companies for the issue of bonds exempt from withholding tax, bank holding companies and management companies for investment funds.[116]

Branches and subsidiaries of banks enjoy particularly favourable conditions. They are not subject to any special restrictions or official control. Luxembourg has neither a central bank nor any minimum reserve requirements. Indeed there are no special laws for the credit system, as for example the banking law in Germany, but only the recommendations of the banking control commission about certain balance-sheet ratios, the observance of which has not been so very strictly enforced.[117] Furthermore capital movements are strictly still free in Luxembourg, by contrast with the restrictions imposed now by most European countries. All the financial transactions are made through the free market, even after the introduction of the dual foreign exchange market in Benelux.[118]

These facts explain why Luxembourg could develop into a Euro-market centre and why foreign banks scrambled to gain a foothold there. The number represented increased from 32 to 52 from 1969 to 1972.[119] Their total assets increased in the same period from Lfr. 136 billions to Lfr. 517 billions.[120] The growth in total assets and in the number of bank establishments continued in 1973.[121]

The international character of Luxembourg is also evidenced in the fact that only about 10 to 20 of the foreign banks participate in local business: almost 80 per cent of the balance-sheet totals of all Luxembourg banks (over Lfr. 600 billions in 1972) come from Euro-currency business.[122] In contrast to London, which dominates the short-term end of the Euro-market, Luxembourg developed into a centre for medium term roll-over credits [123] and Euro-bonds.

With the development of the Euro-bond market the Luxembourg bourse exercised a growing attraction for foreign banks. After the introduction of the American Interest Equalisation Tax a strong international demand for capital was transferred to the Euro-markets, and long-term Euro-loans were issued in growing amounts. In 1968 the value of Euro-bond issues was $3.1 billions, rising to $3.4 billions in 1971 and $5.0 billions in 1972.[124] Half of all Euro-bonds are quoted in Luxembourg. The number of quotations increased from 220 in 1968 to 501 at the end of 1971 and to 590 (including 128 convertible bonds) at end 1972.[125]

At end 1972, 86 per cent of the quotations were of dollar issues.[126] The launching and stock exchange introduction of a Euro-bond loan requires the issue of a prospectus. However, trade in the securities does not have to bear any tax, or other cost, apart from a small brokerage fee.[127] In order to secure a rapid and efficient clearing of bonds traded, several European and American banks in 1970 established a clearing system under the name of CEDEL (Centrale de Livraison de Valeurs Mobilières).[128] *Cedel*'s capital of $1.5 millions at the end of 1972 was held by 89 banks from 15 countries, 450 banks and brokers firms are linked to the system.[129]

e) *Paris*

Paris had developed into a significant centre of the Euro-dollar market, but not into a leading international financial centre. By contrast with the centres described above, French financial markets have historically always been subject to dirigiste policies over the foreign exchange, money and capital markets. The influence of the State dominates all their activities. True, in order to make Paris into an international financial centre which can hold up its head with London, the French government has been anxious for years to improve its qualifications for this role.[130]

The reform of the banking system in 1966/67 was a first step in this direction. The abolition of the sharp distinction between deposit and business banks as well as the lessening of state influence on the banks, for example on their credit and branching policies, resulted in a sharper competitiveness and greater concentration in banking.[131] The idea was to make the banks contribute more effectively to industrial financing: the lack of a proper capital market had meant that companies had had to rely mainly on self-financing for funds to support expansion.

This demand by French industry for medium and long-term finance was indeed one reason for the influx of foreign banks to Paris.[132] At end 1972 foreign banks in France were represented by 34 branches, 28 subsidiaries, 64 representative offices and 20 minority holdings in French institutions.[133] Besides a number of joint subsidiaries were established in which banks from various countries participated. American and British banks have been represented in Paris for many years. They also maintain the largest number of establishments. Continental European banks on the other hand have not been directly represented in Paris, but have now made cooperation agreements with French institutions, or established joint subsidiaries with them.[134] The main business consists as before in servicing the subsidiaries of their own customers established in France, and in making available resources for financing foreign direct investment of French enterprises.[135]

The establishment regulations and the capital requirements imposed on foreign banks are interpreted liberally.[136] Moreover, foreign banks are on the same footing as domestic institutions in their funding activities though in comparison to other markets refinancing through the French money market is more difficult, because the market is so strongly influenced by the Bank of France.[137] Despite these difficulties, foreign banks in the last few years have been able to extend their business in France, funding their activities through close collaboration with local French banks.[138] Beyond this, further facilities were opened to foreign banks as a result of the reform of the Paris money market in 1970. After 1971 refinancing took place not by rediscounting money market papers, but by the open market policies of the Bank of France.[139]

The effort that the French government has made to promote the development of Paris as a financial centre is also evident in the reform of the French bourse. This aims at making investment in French securities more attractive for foreigners. Apart from institutional improvements, at end 1971 the foreign exchange controls were relaxed, so that foreigners could remit freely profits from dealing in securities.[140] Moreover, the 50% tax credit on dividends was extended to all shareholders in the EEC and in countries with which France had concluded double taxation agreements.[141] In order to improve the flow of information required by foreign investors the amount of information that has to be made public by enterprises quoted on the stock exchange was extended.

In order to encourage the further internationalisation of the French capital market, the issuing of public and private loans by foreign investors is also to be facilitated.[142] Previously only a small share of the gross issuing value of loans floated in France had been represented by foreign issuers.[143] Nevertheless, Paris is an important Euro-bond centre.[144] In 1972 Euro-franc bonds were placed to the value of $446 millions.[145] This corresponds to almost 10 per cent of the total volume of Euro-bonds issued in 1972.[146]

Despite all its liberalisation efforts the predeliction of the French government towards frequent restrictive inventions continues and still presents an obstacle to the further development of Paris as a financial centre.

f) *Other European financial centres*

Amsterdam, Brussels and Milan are other relatively important financial centres in Europe. The economies of the Netherlands and Belgium are both traditionally open and internationally orientated. Brussels is the site of several international organisations and the regional location of numerous multinational enterprises. Equally, Amsterdam possesses the head offices of a number of international enterprises. As locations for the banks' foreign investments these financial centres however have so far been sought by foreign banks only to a slight extent. This is partly because the extensive branch networks maintained by domestic banks in both countries mean that opportunities for foreign banks to conduct local banking are limited;

and partly because the required ratios that foreign banks have to maintain between own resources and liabilities or assets are so stiff that international banking business is put at a disadvantage.[147] Amsterdam however has a more international stock exchange and this makes it more attractive to foreign banks and securities companies.

The interest of foreign banks in the Italian market has grown with the increasing industrialisation of the country in the past decade.[148] They are represented predominantly in Milan, the most important financial centre of Italy, and in Rome.[149] Only a few foreign banks maintain subsidiaries or have participations in Italian institutions. The strong state influence on the banking system and the capital market, which so far have been inefficient in meeting industry's requirements, remains today as noticeable as ever.[150]

4.2. The USA region

Up to the introduction of the Interest Equalisation Tax in 1963 and the first voluntary restraint programme for the improvement of the American balance of payments in 1965, the US capital markets played an important part in the provision of medium and long-term funds for European industrial countries. These restrictions isolated the American markets from other foreign markets.[151] However, New York, the most important financial centre in the USA, could be making a strong come-back with the ending of the Interest Equalisation Tax at the beginning of 1974. Apart from this, the vast American domestic market offers numerous business opportunities for foreign banks. As well as the large and strongly diversified money market, the huge securities market is a particular attraction.[152] Entry into the market by foreign banks is not regulated on the federal (i.e. national) level with the exception of the legal regulations about bank holding companies.[153] The regulations governing branching are laid down by the legislation in force in the individual states. Only in three states — New York, Illinois and Massachusetts — may foreign banks establish themselves in any form. Other states impose certain restrictions on the entry of foreign banks, forbid certain kinds of establishment or do not have legislation on the matter.[154]

The desire of foreign banks to be represented in the USA has grown during the 1960s. The largest and longest-established banks are British, Canadian and Japanese institutions.[155] By reason both of the growing foreign direct investments in the USA, of which one third is attributable to European corporations, and of the increasing competition of American banks abroad, continental European banks in particular saw themselves as being forced to have representation in the USA, in order to offer the branches and subsidiaries of their domestic industrial customers as well as the growing number of multinational enterprises there as comprehensive a range of services as possible.

At the end of 1972 almost 80 foreign banks were represented in the USA, with a total of about 430 agencies, branches, subsidiaries and affiliated companies (companies in which an interest is held) as well as representative offices (as against 175 in 1965).[156] Most banks are represented both in New York and in California – in New York because it has the most important American money market and in California because of its growing significance as a domestic market and as the centre for the Far East trade.[157] Of the 430 foreign points of representation, 235 are in New York, of which two thirds are agencies, branches, subsidiaries and affiliates. In California almost 40 agencies, branches and foreign subsidiaries have been established, which maintain almost 100 branches in California, as well as 18 representative offices.[158]

Taken together, the foreign banks had at end 1972 a balance-sheet total of about $25 billions.[159] The biggest share was attributable to the agencies and branches. At end 1972 the assets of the agencies reached a figure of $11 billions, having tripled since 1965.[160] The growth of the branches was even more rapid, assets in the same period having increased four times to about $5 billions.[161] The business of the foreign banks is mainly concerned with market and foreign exchange operations linked to the financing of trade with the USA.[162] The highly-developed New York money market with its various instruments – the most important, apart from commercial paper, bank acceptances, and certificates of deposit being treasury bills – offers numerous investment possibilities for banks with big dollar assets.[163] On the other hand a number of specialised banks exercise interest arbitrage operations between the New York and the Euro-dollar money markets.[164] The money market also offers a means for funding foreign banks' asset portfolios (in addition to those open through parent banks and borrowings from other foreign institutions or from American banks). But a number of foreign banks have recently broadened their range of services beyond the traditional area of trade financing. Some have widened their lending activities; others have founded stockbroking subsidiaries which have direct access to the American stock exchanges and which are also to some extent engaged in domestic issuing business.[165]

4.3. Financial centres in the Far East

In Asia three financial centres of international importance have emerged: Tokyo, Singapore and Hong Kong.

a) *Tokyo*

The recent internationalisation of Japanese financial markets has been a consequence of the large external surplus of the country and the measures introduced in 1969 by the Japanese government to liberalise money and capital movements.[166] This development is mirrored, in the banking sector, both in the fast-expanding network of Japanese bank offices abroad and in the influx of foreign banks to Tokyo since 1969.[167] Before then the number of foreign banks with branches in Tokyo had been virtually constant for many years, as the Japanese Ministry of Finance had not licensed the establishment of new branches of foreign banks.[168] But then the number of foreign banks with branches increased from 18, in 1969, to 23 in 1971 and 35 in 1972.[169] In 1973 a further 6 foreign banks opened branches.[170] Of the 41 foreign banks at end 1973, 15 originated from the USA, 5 from Great Britain, 3 each from France, Korea and Singapore, 2 each from Switzerland, Brazil and Germany and 6 from other countries. Moreover at end 1973 there were 67 foreign representative offices in Japan, compared with about 51 at end 1972.

The growing desire of foreign banks to have a foothold in Tokyo is based upon the observation that this city will continue to develop into one of the most important financial centres of the world. The entire Asian region can be supplied with finance from Tokyo.[171] However, even if Tokyo, by reason of institutional changes and various measures of liberalisation during the last three years, can be called an international market there still exist a number of restrictions on the business activity of the banks.[172]

In the past the business of foreign banks in Tokyo has arisen mainly out of foreign exchange and trade financing. Today these services are provided predominantly by local banks – only about 4 per cent of this business is transacted by foreign banks.[173] This, however, is still a relatively high share compared with the share held by foreign banks in the entire Japanese credit and deposit business, which is put at only about 1.5 per cent or 1 per cent.[174] Banks which were already represented at the beginning of the 1960s were in a favourable position in so far as Japanese enterprises had to have recourse to foreign capital markets (initially through foreign banks) because the Japanese banking system was at the time not ready to meet such demands. Moreover, these banks could to a certain extent grant yen credits to their domestic clients which were established in Japan. This business was, however, relatively limited as the banks could refinance themselves only to a small extent in yen.[175]

With the internationalisation of Japanese financial markets – beginning with the liberalisation of capital imports – the liquidity situation of foreign banks was eased, and was further bolstered by an expansive monetary policy by the Bank of Japan. However, in 1971 the Bank of Japan restricted the inflow of foreign money in an attempt to prevent a revaluation of the yen.[176] The newly-founded banks only received small exchange quotas in yen, so that they had extreme difficulties in carrying on business in yen on the "assets" side of their balance-sheets, especially since they were excluded from recruiting funds on the local money market.[177]

The influx of short-term capital contributed strongly to the normalisation of the Japanese money market.[178] The daily money market formed for the purpose of evening out short-term liquidity positions had in Japan in fact been for many years a market for medium-term money.[179] This resulted from the liquidity shortage experienced by expanding Japanese enterprises. The big Japanese banks were more interested in attracting long-term deposits from the more liquid local banks, in order to finance the credit demands of large industrial enterprises, than in short-term money.[180] Only with increasing liquidity and the introduction of a market for money market paper in 1971 — and a market for long-term money — could the Japanese daily money market develop into a market for short-term money.[181] With the relaxation of the regulations on foreign currency by the Bank of Japan in the spring 1972, under which natives as well as foreigners could open foreign currency accounts, a dollar money market also came into being in Tokyo.[182] This market is an interbank market and is fed by Euro-dollars.[183] Though the Japanese authorities were hesitant in promoting the Tokyo money market, they pushed the growth and internationalisation of the capital market strongly forward. The first yen bonds were issued in 1970 by the Asian Development Bank.[184] In the following years further yen bonds were floated by foreign issuers and after 1972 a private placement market developed too, especially in dollar bonds issued by US borrowers.[185] At the same time Euro-bond placements were coming thick and fast. However, the volume of foreign borrowings in Japan remained small in comparison with domestic borrowers (DM 1.4 billions against DM 150 billions from December 1970 to August 1973.[186] Foreign banks and brokers have not been allowed to participate in underwriting consortia for foreign yen loans.[187] A big obstacle to further internationalisation is posed by the absence of a developed secondary market for trading existing bonds.

An additional step towards the internationalisation of the capital market was the liberalisation of the share market. In the spring of 1970 Japanese investment companies were allowed to buy foreign shares; and institutional investors and private investors have been able to do likewise since 1971.[188] Since the end of 1973 dealing in foreign shares has also been made possible.[189] The introduction of a number of American and European shares was intended for 1974.

b) *Singapore*

The significance of Singapore as an international financial centre was promoted by the formation of the Asian dollar market in 1968. This was established by the Bank of America, the First National City Bank and other foreign banks by agreement with the Government of the Republic of Singapore and can be characterised as an Asian Euro-dollar market.[190] The unit of account is called the Asian Currency Unit (ACU). Banks established in Singapore, which are provided with a special licence from the Monetary Authority of Singapore, can lend foreign money taken in on currency accounts to non-residents.[191] The most important depositing institutions are banks, multinational enterprises, private customers – mainly from Hong Kong, Japan, Taiwan, Indonesia and the Philippines – and central banks in Asia.[192]

Deposits in the Asian-dollar market were initially redeposited on the Euro-dollar market, but since 1971 they have mainly been employed in loans to Asian enterprises and multinational companies as well as for the funding of foreign banks in Asia.[193] The principal currency is the dollar, but European currencies are also used.

With the growth of this market – its volume rose from $ 1 billion at end 1971 to almost $3 billions at end 1972 – many syndicated loans and foreign fixed-interest loans were launched.[194] The pull of Singapore for foreign banks is above all based on the liberal policy of the government with regard to money and capital movements. At the end of 1973, 43 banks were established in Singapore, apart from 11 local banks, and 29 credit institutions maintained representative offices.[195] A further 18 merchant banks and 3 discount houses were active there.[196] The following measures of the government contributed considerably to the internationalisation of this financial centre:[197]

– The State of Singapore imposed no withholding tax on interest payments on Asian-dollar deposits;
– the tax on interest received from loans to non-residents was cut from 40 to 10 per cent;

— minimum reserve requirements on ACU deposits were abolished;
— negotiable Certificates of Deposit were allowed to be denominated in Singapore dollars;
— exports from Singapore could be financed in ACU funds;
— foreign currency proceeds can be kept in foreign currency accounts for three months for use in making payments abroad;
— for foreign currency business of more than 250,000 Singapore dollars the link to the rate of exchange determined by the Association of Banks in Malaysia and Singapore was abolished.

c) *Hong Kong*

Hong Kong is distinguished by a liberal administrative and legal framework for economic activity and very low tax rates.[198] The profits tax is 15 per cent and this, together with the geographical advantages of Hong Kong in the South East Asia area, has a magnetic influence on foreign enterprises. Hong Kong is now clearly an important financial centre. Its position as a banking centre has traditionally been based on the interest of China and Great Britain, which guarantee its existence.[199] Unlike Singapore, Hong Kong has continued to apply a withholding tax on interest payments, at a rate of 15 per cent. This is regarded as a main reason why Hong Kong did not itself develop into the centre of the Asian-dollar market.[200]

Since the banking crisis in 1965 the establishment of new banks or bank branches in Hong Kong has required a licence. But since then no permission has been given—with the exception of the establishment of Barclays Bank International.[201] The number of foreign banks in Hong Kong was increased thereby to 74; in addition, 46 foreign credit institutions maintain representative offices.[202] Moreover, numerous foreign finance companies, merchant banks and some foreign security brokers none of which require special licences, have set up in Hong Kong.[203] The funds—representing mostly fugitive capital—which are flowing increasingly to Hong Kong, are invested mainly in other international financial centres.[204] At the same time large-scale investments in the whole South East Asia area are financed through Hong Kong. The leading borrowers are Japanese enterprises, which have to some considerable extent funded

68

their foreign investments in Hong Kong.[205] Hong Kong's stock exchange, whose fortunes are naturally linked closely to its economic and political development, has also played a significant role in Asian finance.

4.4. Other financial centres

Apart from the oldest financial centre in the Carribean, the Bahamas, in recent years Bermuda, the Cayman Islands, the Netherlands Antilles, and the Channel Islands Jersey and Guernsey, have proved to be attractive places for foreign banks and financing companies to set up shop. This results essentially from tax advantages and the liberal company laws of these islands, and the fact that few impose any restrictions on currency and capital flows.

5

CONCLUSION

The rapidly-growing internationalisation of banking in western industrial countries in recent years has taken place in various ways. While the American banks have been concentrationg predominantly on building worldwide branch networks, European banks have tended to go for new representative offices and the acquisition of stakes in other banks, leaving aside the existing branch networks of French and British banks outside Europe. The Japanese banks for their part have been able, since the liberalisation of the trade and capital transactions, to build up rapidly their foreign representation.

With the accelerated "internationalisation process" in the second half of the 1960s, the joint venture or consortium bank gained increasing significance. Recently it has become clear that, parallel to numerous joint ventures and their regional expansion, European banks—and especially German banks—have also tended increasingly to set up their own branches abroad. This trend will probably be intensified by the growing engagement of industrial corporations in international business, which will increase further the ever-rising volume of foreign business carried on by banks abroad.

In the expansion of their foreign activities, the banks have chosen Europe, the USA and in recent years the Middle and Far East as their prime business centres. Within these areas, leading international financial centres have enjoyed, by reason of their extensive financing and investment possibilities, a special prominence. In this connection the importance of London as the centre of the Euro-markets is obvious. How far the lifting of controls on US capital transactions will affect these markets remains to be seen. It is certain that the Euro-markets, which remain free of restrictions, will continue to provide valued financing and investment alternatives to national finance markets. Apart from the regions and financial centres hitherto preferred, banks could certainly in future consider more favourably new fields for their foreign expansion—e.g. notably the Arab countries, where intense activity is already taking place.

Together with the internationalisation of banking apparent in its physical expansion, an increasing standardization of the range of services offered by banks has developed. At the same time the adoption of new services such as leasing, factoring, and investment services is taking place mostly through the foundation of, or participation in, special institutions and/or through international cooperation in the establishment of consortium banks.

In view of the growing criticism of multinational enterprises, in future the international activities of the banks could become the subject of heated economic and political discussion. An example of this is the criticism recently made of the activities of foreign banks in the USA. It will be necessary to avoid the adoption of one-sided national regulations, if only in order to avoid the danger of a strong reaction in the host countries against the banks concerned. The expansion of banking abroad requires rather the search for compatible solutions—solutions which are not discriminating but which create liberal conditions for the promotion of competition and efficiency in the world's financial system.

NOTES

1. Hans-Eckart Scharrer (ed.): *Förderung privater Direktinvestionen,* Hamburg 1972.

2. Robert M. Weidenhammer, Otto L. Adelberger: *Das Bank- und Börsenwesen in den USA,* Taschenbücher für Geld, Bank und Börse, No. 32, Frankfurt 1966; Jack M. Guttentag, Edward S. Herman: *Banking structure and performance,* New York 1967; Hartmut Schmidt: Vereinigte Staaten von Amerika, in *Blätter für Genossenschaftswesen,* Vol. 117 (1971) No. 19/20, p. 416 ff.; and Alfred R. Bennett: American Commercial Banking: The Changing Scene, in *Lloyds Bank Review,* No. 101, July 1971, p. 39 ff.

3. Maximum interest rates are applicable to time deposit accounts and certificates of deposit; current account deposits may not bear interest.

4. Mary Campbell: The Multinational Banking Framework, in *The Banker,* Vol. 121, No. 544 (June 1971) p. 629.

5. U.S. Banks, Scope for expansion overseas, in *The Financial Times,* No. 23328 (June 3, 1964); and George Bolton: American banks spread world branches, in *The Times,* London, No. 56935 (May 8, 1967).

6. Dietmar Haubold: *Direktinvestitionen und Zahlungsbilanz,* Hamburg 1972; and Entwicklung und Förderung der amerikanischen Direktinvestitionen, in Hans-Eckart Scharrer (ed.), *op. cit.;* Otto G. Mayer: *Direktinvestitionen und Wachstum,* Hamburg 1973; and Sabine von Saldern: *Internationaler Vergleich der Direktinvestitionen wichtiger Industrieländer,* HWWA-Report No. 15, Hamburg 1973, p. 24 ff.

7. US Banks' Stake Abroad Heads for $200 Billion, in *The Journal of Commerce,* International Banking Issue, Twelfth Annual Edition, Vol. 322, No. 23, 341 (Dec. 9, 1974) p. 1.

8. Dietmar Haubold: Entwicklung und Förderung der amerikanischen Direktinvestitionen, *op. cit.,* p. 97 ff.; and Sabine von Saldern, *op. cit.,* p. 27.

9. See Recent Activities of Foreign Branches of U.S. Banks, in *Federal Reserve Bulletin* (October 1972) p. 855 ff.; and Overseas Branches of Member Banks, in *Federal Reserve Bulletin* (September 1971) p. 757 f.

10. Edge Act corporations are established according to federal law especially for holding participations in banks and/or other companies abroad.

11. Peter Brunsden: The Edge Act in U.S. Banking, in *The Banker*, Vol. 123, No. 564 (February 1973) p. 149.

12. Klaus Engelen: US-Banken im Ausland sehr dynamisch, in *Handelsblatt*, No. 203 (Oct. 21, 1968); also see Edge Act Affiliates of Banks Grow and Prosper, in *The Journal of Commerce*, New York, No. 22589 (Dec. 13, 1971); and New Horizons Open for US Banking Overseas, in *The Journal of Commerce*, New York, No. 22842 (Dec. 11, 1972).

13. Peter Brunsden, *op. cit.*

14. See Notebook Britain, US banks in London, in *The Banker*, Vol. 123, No. 567 (May 1973) p. 449 f.

15. Nicholas Colchester: Dollar on the defensive, in *The Financial Times*, No. 25769 (May 30, 1972).

16. Bank of America, First National City Bank, Chase Manhattan Bank, Morgan Guaranty Trust Co., Manufacturers Hanover Trust, Chemical Bank, Bankers Trust.

17. Edward P. Foldessy: Branching Out – U.S. Banks Find Money in Offices Abroad, Foreign Profit Gains Outpace Home Results, in *The Wall Street Journal*, New York, No. 104 (May 26, 1972).

18. William Hall: Remember the Summer of '74?, in *The Banker*, Vol. 125, No. 591 (May 1975) p. 537.

19. Edward P. Foldessy, *op. cit.*

20. For example the greater part of the net value of British direct investment overseas is in the Commonwealth countries of the old sterling area. Since 1960 the share of these countries has declined as that of other countries – above all the United States and the EEC countries – has risen. See Klaus Boeck: Entwicklung und Förderung der britischen Direktinvestitionen, in Hans Eckart Scharrer (ed.), *op. cit.*, p. 240 ff.

21. Manfred Hein: Strukturanalysen ausländischer Bankensysteme: Grossbritannien, in Erich Thiess (ed.): *Schriftenreihe des Instituts für Bank und Kreditwirtschaft der Freien Universität Berlin*, No. 1, Frankfurt/Main 1967, p. 10 ff; Robin Pringle, *Banking in Britain*, London 1973.

22. Bernd Küppers: Zur Bankenkonzentration in Grossbritannien, in *Sparkasse*, Vol. 85 (1968) No. 10, p. 155 ff; Rudolf Hahn: Konzentration im Kreditgewerbe: England I, Schritte auf dem Weg zur Universalbank, in *Handelsblatt*, No. 77 (April 19, 1968); and England II, Rationalisierung ist Trumpf, in *Handelsblatt*, No. 78 (April 22, 1968).

23. Bernd Küppers, *op. cit.*, p. 157.

24. New strength for British banking abroad, in *The Times*, London, No. 56076 (July 29, 1964).

25. Lord Aldington: Operating abroad from a home base, in *The Times*, London, No. 57842 (April 13, 1970).

26. Ian Morrison: Retreat from the third world, in *The Times*, London. No. 58150 (April 19, 1971).

27. Cadogan A. Gordon: British Banking in New York, in *The Banker*, Vol. 119. No. 521 (July 1969) p. 673.

28. Richard Fry: British banks with a stake in America, in *The Times*, London, No. 57477 (February 5, 1969).

29. Before the merger of Lloyds Bank Europe and BOLSA, Mellon Bank was the second largest shareholder in BOLSA after Lloyds Bank. Lloyds & Bolsa International Bank Ltd. became a wholly owned subsidiary of Lloyds Bank Ltd. in 1973. The name of this subsidiary was changed to Lloyds Bank International Ltd. in April 1974.

30. Midland's International Role, in *The Financial Times*, No. 25591 (Oct. 29, 1971).

31. Sandra Mason: Merchant banking today and in future, in *Journal of Business Finance*, Vol. 3 (1971) No. 4, p. 9; and Cees F. Scheffer, *The present and future of the London merchant banks*, SUERF Series 15 A, Tilburg 1974.

32. Sandra Mason, *ibid.*

33. Sandra Mason, *op. cit.*, p. 6 ff; and D. V. Bendall: Leichte Kavallerie — Britische "merchant banks" und ihre Rolle, in *Die Welt*, No. 118 (May 24, 1972).

34. Enge Kontakte der Großbanken mit London, in *Frankfurter Allgemeine Zeitung*, No. 265 (Nov. 14, 1973).

35. On the internationalisation of German industry see Rolf Jungnickel, Georg Koopmann, Klaus Matthies, Rolf Sutter, (ed. by Manfred Holthus): *Die deutschen multinationalen Unternehmen*, Frankfurt 1974; Rolf Jungnickel, Georg Koopmann: Wie multinational sind die deutschen Unternehmen?, in *Wirtschaftsdienst*, Vol. 52 (1972) No. 4, p. 191; and Im Ausland auf dem Vormarsch, in *Manager Magazin*, No. 12 (1973) p. 116.

36. Henry Krägenau: Entwicklung und Förderung der deutschen Direktinvestitionen, in Hans-Eckart Scharrer (ed.), *op. cit.*, p. 486; and Sabine von Saldern, *op. cit.*, p. 75.

37. Hanns Kippenberger: 'Nach acht Jahren Erfahrung kann man sagen, daß die Hauptgründe, die zum Entstehen dieser internationalen Banken führten, auch heute noch voll oder sogar in verstärktem maße gültig sind', in *Handelsblatt*, survey, International Banking, No. 215 (Nov. 9, 1971) p. XIX f.

38. Orion Termbank Ltd. took over the share capital of Orion Bank Ltd. and changed its name into Orion Bank Ltd. The merger became effective on December 30, 1974.

39. Hanns Kippenberger, *op. cit.*

40. Ken Gooding: Consortia concepts, in *The Financial Times*, No. 26036 (April 16, 1973).

41. Deutsche Bank AG: Geschäftsbericht für das Jahr 1972, p. 43.

42. Hanns Kippenberger, *op. cit.*, p. XX.

43. Mammut-Tanker und Büromaschinen von Orion, in *Handelsblatt*, No. 15 (Jan. 22, 1973).

44. In 1973 the Banco de Comercio S.A. (Mexico) and in 1974 the Banco Itaú S.A. (Brazil) became shareholders of Libra.

45. See Banken — Feine Töchter in Luxemburg, in *Wirtschaftswoche*, No. 15 (April 6, 1973), and *Nachrichten für Aussenhandel*, No. 80 (April 24, 1973).

46. Deutsche Bank AG: Geschäftsbericht für das Jahr 1972, p. 42 f.

47. Commerzbank AG: Geschäftsbericht für das Jahr 1972, p. 53.

48. Deutsche Bank AG: Geschäftsbericht für das Jahr 1972, p. 44.

49. Karl-Georg Schmidt: Deutsche Banken in Entwicklungsländern, in *Bank-Betrieb*, Vol. 6 (1966) No. 9, p. 225.

50. Total assets 1972 DM 1,114.5 millions against DM 753.9 millions in 1971. Annual report of the Deutsche Ueberseeische Bank.

51. See annual report, 1972, of the Deutsch-Südamerikanische Bank and the Deutsche Ueberseeische Bank.

52. Albert Dormanns: Deutsche Banken im Ausland, in *Bank-Betrieb*, Vol. 10 (1970) No. 1, p. 3.

53. Henri Fournier: Frankreich, in *Blätter für Genossenschaftswesen*, Sonderausgabe: Kreditwesen — Entwicklungstendenzen in acht Ländern, Vol. 117 (1971) No. 19/20, p. 369.

54. Henri Fournier, *op. cit.;* and Jonathan Radice: French Banking, in *The Banker*, Vol. 123, No. 563 (January 1973) p. 51.

55. Paris fusioniert zwei verstaatlichte Banken, in *Frankfurter Allgemeine Zeitung*, No. 105 (May 6, 1966).

56. Rudolphe Hottinguer: International business, in *The Banker*, Vol. 123, No. 563 (January 1973) p. 53.

57. *Ibid.*, p. 53.

58. Suez: Ein Kauf für Mutige, in *Finanz und Wirtschaft*, No. 13 (February 17, 1973).

59. Yves Marcille: Les relations bancaires Franco-Belges, in *Revue Banque,* No. 315 (February 1973) p. 111.

60. Adrian Dicks: Latest results are surprisingly healthy, in *The Financial Times,* Financial Times Survey on World Banking XXV, France, No. 25774 (June 5, 1972); and: Merchant banks, Paribas on display, in *The Economist,* Vol. 247, No. 6773 (June 1973) p. 106.

61. Merchant banks, *op. cit.;* and Robert Mauthner: Tough going in constant bid to counter inflation, in *The Financial Times,* Financial Times Survey on World Banking VII, France, No. 26036 (April 16, 1973).

62. Französische Bankinteressen in den USA, in *Neue Zürcher Zeitung,* No. 175 (June 28, 1972).

63. *Ibid,* and: La b.n.p. au Japon, in *L'Usine Nouvelle,* No. 15 (April 12, 1973).

64. T. F. M. Adams, Iwao Hoshii: *A Financial History of the New Japan,* Tokyo, Palo Alto 1972, p. 91; and Bernd Baehring: *Weltfinanz im Fernen Osten,* Frankfurt/Main 1973, p. 80.

65. T. F. M. Adams, Iwao Hoshii, *op. cit.,* p. 468.

66. Albrecht Dormanns: Japans Banken an der Schwelle zu einer neuen Entwicklung, in *Bank-Betrieb,* Vol. 13 (1973) No. 3, p. 86.

67. Ichiro Takeuchi: Japanese Banks Overseas, in *The Bankers' Magazine,* Vol. 204 (1967) No. 1483, p. 173.

68. Manfred Holthus: Entwicklung und Förderung der japanischen Direktinvestitionen, in Hans-Eckart Scharrer (ed.), *op. cit.,* p. 401; and Sabine von Saldern, *op. cit.,* p. 59.

69. Ichiro Takeuchi: Expansion of Japanese banking abroad, in *Euromoney,* Japan – the rising force in international banking (March 1973) p. 3. .

70. T. Komatsubara: Overseas activities of Japanese banks, in *The Banker,* Vol. 120, No. 531 (May 1970) p. 474.

71. Ichiro Takeuchi: Expansion of Japanese banking abroad, *op. cit.*

72. T. F. M. Adams, Iwao Hoshii, *op. cit.,* p. 474.

73. Multinationalization of Japanese Firms – (4), Banking & Securities, in *The Oriental Economist,* Vol. 41 (1973) No. 748, p. 25.

74. See *ibid.*

75. Ichiro Takeuchi: Expansion of Japanese banking abroad, *op. cit.,* p. 4.

76. Helmut Haeusgen: Singapur wächst zu bedeutender Kapitaldrehscheibe Asiens heran, in. *Handelsblatt,* No. 220 (Nov. 14, 1972); T. H. Attwood: Singapore – The Asian Dollar Market, in *Euromoney* (March 1972) p. 56.

77. T. F. M. Adams, Iwao Hoshii, *op. cit.,* p. 473.

78. Ichiro Takeuchi, Japanese banks overseas in 1974, *op. cit.*, p. 63.

79. Ernst Neubronner: Die europäischen Finanzzentren, in *Blätter für Genossenschaftswesen,* Vol. 118 (1972) No. 24, p. 405; and Max Iklé: Die Schweiz als internationaler kapitalmarkt, in R. F. Behrendt, W. Müller, H. Sieber, M. Weber (eds.): *Strukturwandlungen der Schweizerischen Wirtschaft und Gesellschaft,* Bern 1962, p. 251.

80. Ernst Neubronner: *op. cit.,* p. 405 f.

81. Ernst Neubronner, *op. cit.,* p. 405; George Williamson: Finanzplatz London, in Schweizerische Kreditanstalt: *Bulletin,* Vol. 78 (July 1972) p. 18; and Mary Ling: Will the British banks confront, compete or cooperate?, in *Commerce International,* The Journal of the London Chamber of Commerce and Industry, No. 1401 (January 1973) p. 10.

82. Christopher Gwinner: Why U.S. banks come to London, in *The Financial Times,* No. 24529 (May 1, 1968); George Williamson, *op. cit.,* Mary Ling, *op. cit.,* and William M. Clarke: The City's foreign business: role of the banks, in *Euromoney* (December 1972), p. 13.

83. Christopher Gwinner, *op. cit.;* and William M. Clarke, *op. cit.*

84. The record of the past 12 months, in *The Banker,* Vol. 122, No. 561 (November 1972) p. 1453.

85. *Ibid.*

86. Bank of England: *Quarterly Bulletin.*

87. *Ibid.*

88. Bank of England: *Quarterly Bulletin.*

89. Developments in Eurodollar business, in *The Banker,* Vol. 122, No. 561 (November 1972) p. 1433.

90. OECD: *Financial Statistics,* 6, Tome I (December 1972) p. 405.

91. *Ibid.*

92. E. Reinhardt: *Switzerland—International Finance Center,* Swiss Credit Bank, Zürich, 1966, p. 3.

93. Max Iklé: Swiss invisible earnings, in *The Banker,* Vol. 123, No. 564 (February 1973) p. 188.

94. *Ibid.*

95. *Ibid.*

96. Fritz Zimmermann: Auslandsbanken in der Schweiz, in *Der Schweizer Treuhänder,* Vol. 47 (1973) No. 2, p. 38.

97. Fritz Zimmermann, *op. cit.,* p. 38.

98. Mary Campbell: A leading place in the international scene, in *The Financial Times,* No. 26095 (June 28, 1973).

99. Ernst Neubronner, *op. cit.*, p. 406.

100. Fritz Zimmermann, *op. cit.*, p. 39 f.

101. John Wicks: The gnomes of Zurich and elsewhere, in *The Financial Times*, No. 26095 (June 28, 1973).

102. Alfred Schäfer: Die internationalen Kapitalmärkte aus schweizerischer Sicht, in *Zeitschrift für das Gesamte Kreditwesen*, Vol. 22 (1969) No. 24, p. 1157.

103. Alfred Schäfer, *op. cit.*, p. 1157; and Ernst Neubronner, *op. cit.*, p. 407.

104. R. Lang: Das Emissionsgeschäft in der Schweiz und im Ausland, in Schweizerische Kreditanstalt: *Bulletin*, Vol. 79 (April/Mai 1973) p. 10.

105. OECD, *Financial Statistics*, *op. cit.*, p. 405.

106. *Ibid.*

107. Deutsche Bundesbank: Die Zweigstellen ausländischer Banken in der Bundesrepublik, in *Monatsberichte der Deutschen Bundesbank*, Vol. 24 (1972) No. 4, p. 208.

108. *Ibid.*

109. *Ibid.*, p. 209; and Bundesministerium der Finanzen: *Finanznachrichten*, No. 4/1973 (Sept. 14, 1973).

110. Bundesministerium der Finanzen, *op. cit.*

111. Deutsche Bundesbank, *op. cit.*, p. 209; and Bundesministerium der Finanzen, *op. cit.*

112. Deutsche Bundesbank, *op. cit.*, p. 210 ff.

113. Gottfried Glow: Luxemburg als Finanz- und Bankplatz, in *Österreichisches Bank-Archiv*, Vol. 20 (1972) No. 12, p. 434.

114. *Ibid.*, and Bernd Baehring: Luxemburg—"An ally of the City", in *The Banker*, Vol. 123, No. 568 (June 1973) p. 582.

115. Bernd Baehring, *op. cit.*

116. *Ibid.*

117. Gottfried Glow, *op. cit.*, p. 435.

118. Ernest Muhlen: Das Grossherzogtum sprengt engräumige kapitalmärkte, in Ministère d'Etat. Service Information et Presse: *Bulletin de documentation* (1973) No. 1, p. 9.

119. Bernd Baehring, *op. cit.*, p. 583.

120. *Ibid.*

121. *Ibid.*

122. *Ibid.*

123. Ernst Neubronner, *op. cit.*, p. 408.

124. Henri Grisius: An der Börse werden fast 600 Euroanleihen notiert, in *Bulletin de documentation, op. cit.*, p. 12.

125. Bernd Baehring, *op. cit.*, p. 582; and Ernst Neubronner, *op. cit.*, p. 408.

126. Henri Grisius, *op. cit.*, p. 13.

127. Gottfried Glow, *op. cit.*, p. 436.

128. Clearing systems, in *The Financial Times*, No. 25398 (March 8, 1971).

129. Edmond Israel, Clearing-Stelle erleichtert den Handel mit Effekten, in *Bulletin de documentation, op. cit.*, p. 11.

130. Mary Campbell: Widespread increase in international operations, in *The Financial Times*, No. 26190 (Oct. 18, 1973).

131. Richard Fry: A brisk awakening, in *The Banker*, Vol. 123, No. 563 (January 1973) p. 41 f.

132. Hervé de Carmoy: Foreign Banks, in *The Banker*, Vol. 123, No. 563 (January 1973) p. 58 f.

133. Foreign Banks in France, in *The Banker*, Vol. 123, No. 563 (January 1973) p. 79 ff.

134. Hervé de Carmoy, *op. cit.*, p. 59.

135. Mary Campbell, Widespread increase in international operations, *op. cit.*

136. Hervé de Carmoy, *op. cit.*, p. 59.

137. *Ibid.*

138. *Ibid.*

139. Neue Etappe in der Reform des Pariser Geldmarktes, in *Neue Zürcher Zeitung*, No. 210 (August 4, 1973).

140. Ernst Neubronner, *op. cit.*, p. 407; and Interview M. Giscard d'Estaing, in *The Banker*, Vol. 123, No. 563 (January 1973) p. 45 f.

141. *Ibid.*

142. Giscard hat nichts mehr gegen Auslandsanleihen, in *Handelsblatt*, No. 11 (January 16, 1973).

143. Ernst Neubronner, *op. cit.*, p. 408.

144. Rupert Cornwall: Role of Paris in financial world, in *The Financial Times*, No. 26057 (May 14, 1973).

145. Attention, the Ides of March, International Banking, in *The Economist*, Vol. 246 (1973) No. 6753, p. 43.

146. *Ibid.*

147. Mary Campbell: Brussels — Service Centre for European Finance, in *The Banker,* Vol. 122, No. 554 (April 1972) p. 485 ff.; and: Facing up to a time of change, in *The Financial Times,* Survey: Dutch Capital Markets, No. 26304 (March 5, 1974); and: The impact of foreign banks, in *The Financial Times,* No. 25954 (Jan. 10, 1973).

148. Antonio Tonello: Foreign Banks in Italy, in *The Banker,* Vol. 121, No. 545 (July 1971), p. 824 ff.

149. See *ibid.*

150. Richard Fry: The financial "miracle" is still to come, in *The Banker,* Vol. 121, No. 545 (July 1971) p. 783 f.

151. J. Arthur Urcinoli: The U.S. capital market as a source of funds for international issuers, in *Euromoney* (September 1973) p. 4.

152. Fred H. Klopstock: Foreign Banks in the United States: Scope and Growth of Operations in Federal Reserve Bank of New York, *Monthly Review,* Vol. 55 (1973) No. 6, p. 141.

153. Ward C. Krebs: Foreign Banks in California — and the U.S., in *Euromoney* (December 1973) p. 60.

154. Ward C. Krebs, *op.cit.,* p. 60.

155. Richard P. Cooley: *Foreign Bank Activity in the United States,* Association of Reserve City Banking, Annual Meeting, Boca Raton, Florida (April 10, 1973) p. 3.

156. Fred H. Klopstock, *op.cit.,* p. 142; and Richard P. Cooley, *op.cit.,* p. 1.

157. Richard P. Cooley, *op.cit.,* p. 1.

158. Richard P. Cooley, *op.cit.,* p. 5 and 7.

159. Fred H. Klopstock, *op.cit.,* p. 143.

160. Fred H. Klopstock, *op.cit.,* p. 142 f.

161. *Ibid.*

162. Fred H. Klopstock, *op.cit.,* p. 143.

163. Fred H. Klopstock, *op.cit.,* p. 141; and Peter J. Brunsden: The money markets: a guide, in *The Banker,* Vol. 123, No. 571 (September 1973) p. 1031.

164. Fred H. Klopstock, *op.cit.,* p. 146 f.

165. Fred H. Klopstock, *op.cit.,* p. 142 f. and p. 149 f.

166. Tadahiro Asami: Der japanische Kapitalmarkt, Die jüngsten Entwicklungen, in *Finanzierung und Entwicklung,* Vol. 9 (1972) No. 4, p. 53 f.

167. G. Denham, E. Chaloner: The prospects for foreign financial institutions in Japan, in *Euromoney* (March 1973) p. 25.

168. *Ibid.*

169. *Ibid.*

170. J. R. Drumwright: Foreign banks grow despite funding problems, in *Euromoney:* International banking in Japan – a survey (March 1974) p. 31.

171. G. Denham, E. Chaloner, *op. cit.,* p. 25; and Robert L. Davidson: Foreign Banks – a crowded road to Tokyo, in *The Banker,* Vol. 123, No. 569 (July 1973) p. 807.

172. Robert L. Davidson, *op. cit.*; and Tatsuo Shinoki: Changes in the Tokyo capital market – and its problems, in *Euromoney* (March 1973) p. 15.

173. Robert L. Davidson, *op. cit.,* p. 811.

174. *Ibid.*

175. G. Denham, E. Chaloner, *op. cit.,* p. 26.

176. Robert L. Davidson, *op. cit.,* p. 811.

177. *Ibid*; and G. Denham, E. Chaloner, *op. cit.,* p. 26.

178. Seiichi Nishiyama: The Japanese money market and capital flows, in *Euromoney* (March 1973), p. 21.

179. Seiichi Nishiyama, *op. cit.,* p. 23.

180. *Ibid.*

181. *Ibid.*

182. G. Denham, E. Chaloner, *op. cit.,* p. 26; and Akira Kojima: Japans Kapitalkontrollen sind weitgehend abgebaut, in *Handelsblatt:* Finanzzentren in Asien, No. 238 (Dec. 11, 1973).

183. Paul von Benckendorff: Tokio könnte zum London des Ostens werden, in *Handelsblatt:* Finanzzentren in Asien, No. 238 (Dec. 11, 1973).

184. G. Denham, E. Chaloner, *op. cit.,* p. 27.

185. *Ibid*; and Tatsuo Shinoki, *op. cit.,* p. 15.

186. Paul von Benckendorff, *op. cit.,* p. 20.

187. *Ibid.*

188. Tadashi Ishida: Der Internationalisierung des Tokioter Kapitalmarktes steht noch eine Reihe von Hindernissen im Weg, in *Handelsblatt:* Finanzzentren in Asien, No. 238 (Dec. 11, 1973).

189. Tadashi Ishida, *op. cit.*

190. S. Venu: A Note on the Asian Dollar Market, in *The Bankers' Magazine,* Vol. 216, No. 1514 (September 1973) p. 117.

191. Franz Schrott: Finanzplätze in aller Welt, Singapur, in *Zeitschrift für das gesamte Kreditwesen,* Vol. 26 (1973) No. 23, p. 1154.

192. S. Venu, *op. cit.,* p. 117; and: The Asian Dollar Market in Singapore, in Moscow Narodny Bank: *Quarterly Review,* Vol. 80 (1973) No. 14, p. 35 ff.

193. Franz Schrott, *op. cit.*, p. 1154; The Asian Dollar Market in Singapore, *op. cit.*; and Raymond A. Kathe: Asiadollar Market, Benefits in Lending, in *Far Eastern Economic Review*, Vol. 80 (1973) No. 14, p. 35 ff.

194. The Asian Dollar Market in Singapore, *op. cit.*, p. 25 f.

195. Franz Schrott, *op.cit.*, p. 1154.

196. *Ibid.*

197. *Ibid*; and: Singapur, internationale Drehscheibe des Asien-Dollar-Marktes, in *Handelsblatt:* Finanzzentren in Asien, No. 238 (Dec. 11, 1973).

198. Otto Wendt: Finanzplätze in aller Welt, Hongkong, in *Zeitschrift für das gesamte Kreditwesen*, Vol. 26 (1973) No. 23, p. 1146.

199. Stewart Dalby: A centre in its own right, in *The Financial Times, Financial Times Survey: World Banking XX*, No. 26036 (April 16, 1973).

200. Otto Wendt, *op. cit.*

201. Richard Fry: Hongkong-aftermath and prospects, in *The Banker*, Vol. 123, No. 568 (June 1973) p. 538.

202. Richard Fry: Hongkong — aftermath and prospect, *op.cit.*, p. 558.

203. Richard Fry: Hongkong — aftermath and prospect, *op. cit.*, p. 558 f.; and Otto Wendt, *op. cit.*

204. Stewart Dalby, *op.cit.;* and Otto Wendt, *op. cit.*

205. Richard Fry: Hongkong — aftermath and prospect, *op. cit.*, p. 560; and Otto Wendt, *op.cit.*

APPENDIX 1

The main consortium banks and co-operative ventures

Year of establishment	Name	Head office	Capital	France
1964	Midland and International Bank Ltd., "MAIBL"	London	10 Mill. £	
1967	Banque Européenne de Crédit, "BEC" [1]	Brussels	1,332 Mill. bfrs	Société Générale (13.12)
	International Commercial Bank Ltd., "ICB"	London	5 Mill. £	Crédit Lyonnais (11)
	Martin Corporation Group Ltd.	Sydney	6 Mill. A $	
	SociétéFinancière Européenne, "SFE"	Luxembourg	160 Mill. sfrs	Banque Nationale de Paris (12.5)
	Banque de la Société Financière Européenne "BSFE"	Paris	100 Mill. FF	Banque Nationale de Paris (6)

Participating banks (with % held)

-many	*Italy*	*Britain*	*USA*	*Other countries*
		Midland Bank Ltd. (45); Standard Bank Ltd. (19)		Commercial Bank of Australia Ltd. (10); Toronto-Dominion Bank (26)
ᴊtsche Bank (13.12)	Banca Commerciale Italiana (13.12)	Midland Bank Ltd. (13.12); Samuel Montagu & Co. Ltd. (8.14)		Société Générale de Banque S.A. (13.12); Amsterdam-Rotterdam Bank N.V. (13.12); Creditanstalt-Bankverein, Wien (13.12)
ᴎmerzbank (12)	Banco di Roma (11)		First National Bank of Chicago (22); Irving Trust Company (22)	The Hongkong and Shanghai Banking Corp., Hongkong (22)
		Bearings Brothers (20); United Dominions Trust Ltd. (40)	Wells Fargo Bank (40)	
sdner Bank (12.5)	Banca Nazionale del Lavoro (12.5)	Barclays Bank Ltd. (12.5)	Bank of America (12.5)	Algemene Bank Nederland N.V. (12.5); Banque de Bruxelles S.A. (12.5); Sumitomo Bank Ltd. (12.5)
sdner Bank (6)	Banca Nazionale del Lavoro (6)	Barclays Bank Ltd. (6)	Bank of America (6)	Algemene Bank Nederland N.V. (6); Banque de Bruxelles S.A. (6); Sumitomo Bank Ltd. (6) Société Financière Européenne (52)

Year of estab-lishment	Name	Head office	Capital	France
1968	European-American Banking Corporation, "EABC"[2]	New York	19 Mill. US $	Société Géné-rale (20.125)
	European-American Bank & Trust Com-pany, "EABTC"[3]	New York	60 Mill. US $	Société Géné-rale (18.375)
	Intercontinental Banking Services (Beratungsgesell-schaft)	London	3.5 Mill. £	
	Western American Bank (Europe) Ltd.	London	4.5 Mill. £	
1969	Atlantic Interna-tional Bank Ltd.	London	4 Mill. £	

88

		Participating banks (with % held)		
~many	*Italy*	*Britain*	*USA*	*Other countries*
₁tsche Bank (20.125)		Midland Bank Ltd. (20.125)		Amsterdam-Rotterdam Bank N.V. (17); Société Générale de Banque S.A. (20.125); Creditanstalt-Bankverein, Wien (2.5)
₁tsche Bank (18.375)		Midland Bank Ltd. (18.375)	European-American Banking Corporation (18.375)	Amsterdam-Rotterdam Bank N.V. (15.522); Société Générale de Banque S.A. (18.375); Creditanstalt-Bankverein, Wien (2.283)
		Barclays Bank Ltd. (14.3); The Chartered Bank (14.3); Lloyds Bank (14.3); Lloyds & Bolsa (14.3); Barclays DCO (14.3)		Australia and New Zealand Bank (14.3); National Bank of New Zealand (14.3)
		Hambros Bank Ltd. (10)	National Bank of Detroit (22.5); Security Pacific National Bank (22.5); Wells Fargo Bank (22.5)	The Bank of Tokyo Ltd. (22.5)
	Banco di Napoli (16.66)	Charterhouse Japhet Ltd. (16.66)	Manufacturers National Bank of Detroit (25) National Shawmut Bank of Boston (25)	F. van Lanschot Bankiers, 's-Hertogenbosch (16.66)

89

Year of estab- lishment	Name	Head office	Capital	France
1969	Banque Occidentale pour l'Industrie et le Commerce	Paris	32,058 Mill. FF	Générale Occidentale (80)
	Manufacturers Hanover Ltd.	London	1.25 Mill. £	
	Rothschild Intercontinental Bank Ltd., "RIB"	London	5.52 Mill. £	Banque Rothschild S.A.[4]
	Union Internationale de Financement et de Participation, "INTERUNION-Banque"	Paris	36 Mill. FF	Sté. Financière Desmarais pour l'Industrie et le Commerce (9.7); Banque de l'Union Européenne Industrielle et Financière; Compagnie Financière de L'Union Européenne (together 19.52)

rmany	Italy	Britain	USA	Other countries
			Central National Bank of Cleveland (10); Union Bank of Los Angeles (10)	
	Riunione Adriatica di Sicurta (10)	N. M. Rothschild & Sons (10)	Manufacturers Hanover Trust (75)	Long Term Credit Bank of Japan (5)
. Oppen- m jr. & :. (6.17)		N. M. Rothschild & Sons[4]; Eagle Star Insurance Group (2.883)	First City National Bank of Houston (11.367); National City Bank of Cleveland (11.367); Seattle First National Bank (11.367)	Industrial Bank of Japan (11.367); Banque Privée S.A., Genf[4]; Banque Lambert S.C.S.[4]; Pierson Heldring and Pierson[4]
yerische reinsbank 7)	La Centrale Financiaria Generale S.p.A. (4.73)		Marine Midland Bank Inc. (19.4)	Banque de Bruxelles S.A. (9.7); Banque Belge pour l'Industrie (4.82); Royal Bank of Canada International Ltd., Nassau (9.7); Banque Commerciale de Bâle, Basel (2.63); Hambros Bank Ltd. (4.84); The Tokai Bank Ltd. (5.26)

91

Year of establishment	Name	Head office	Capital	France
1970	Australian European Finance Corporation Ltd.	Sydney	5 Mill. A-$	Banque Nationale de Paris (23)
	European Banks' International Company S.A., "EBIC"	Brussels	175 Mill. bfrs	Société Générale (14.3)
	Euro-Pacific Finance Corporation Ltd., "EPEC"	Melbourne	2.5 Mill. A-$	Société Générale (8)
	London Multinational Bank Ltd.	London	4 Mill. £	
	Internationale Bank für Außenhandel AG	Wien	75 Mill. öS	Banque Worms (5)

ermany	Italy	Britain	USA	Other countries
resdner Bank G (18)	Banca Nazionale del Lavoro (18)			Algemene Bank Nederland N.V. (18); Commonwealth Trading Bank of Australia (23)
eutsche Bank G (14.3)	Banca Commerciale Italiana (14.3)	Midland Bank Ltd. (14.3)		Amsterdam-Rotterdam Bank N.V. (14.3); Société Générale de Banque S.A. (14.3); Creditanstalt-Bankverein, Wien (14.3)
eutsche Bank G (8)		Midland Bank Ltd. (15.5)	United California Bank (12.5)	Amsterdam-Rotterdam Bank N.V. (8); Société Générale de Banque S.A. (8); Commercial Bank of Australia Ltd. (25); The Fuji Bank Ltd. (15)
		Baring Brothers (20)	Chemical Bank (30); Northern Trust Company of Chicago (20)	Schweizerische Kreditanstalt (30)
essische Landesbank-Girozentrale 5)			Philadelphia International Investment Corporation (10)	Bankenkommanditgesellschaft Winter & Co., Wien (25); Genossenschaftliche Zentralbank AG, Wien (12);

93

Year of estab-lishment	Name	Head office	Capital	France
1970				
	United International Bank Ltd.	London	4 Mill. £	Banque Français du Commerce Extérieur (10); Crédit du Nord (10)
	Euro Partners Securities Corporation	New York	3 Mill. US-$	Crédit Lyonnais (33.33)
	Orion Bank Ltd.[7]	London	10 Mill. £	
	Orion Termbank Ltd.[7]	London	12.5 Mill. £	
	Orion Multinational Services Ltd.	London	450 £	
1971	Noreco Finanz AG	Zürich	20 Mill. sfrs	

94

	Participating banks (with % held)			
?rmany	Italy	Britain	USA	Other countries
				Österreichische Credit-Institut AG, Wien (8); Bank für Arbeit und Wirtschaft, Wien (5); Banco de Vizcaya, Madrid (5); Others (5)
ayerische Hy-theken- und echselbank 0)		Williams & Glyn's Bank Ltd. (10)	Crocker-Citizens National Bank (10)	Bank Mees en Hope (10); Bank of Nova Scotia, Halifax (10); Privatbanken i Kjobenhavn A.S. (10); Sveriges Kreditbank (10); Banco de Bilbao (10)
ommerzbank G (33.33)	Banco di Roma (33.33)			
estdeutsche ndesbank-rozentrale 0)	Credito Italiano S.p.A. (10)	National Westminster Bank Ltd. (20)	Chase Manhattan Overseas Banking Corporation (20)	Royal Bank of Canada (20); Mitsubishi Bank Ltd. (10)
estdeutsche ndesbank-rozentrale 0)	Credito Italiano S.p.A. (10)	National Westminster Bank Ltd. (20)	Chase Manhattan Overseas Banking Corporation (20)	Royal Bank of Canada (20); Mitsubishi Bank Ltd. (10)
estdeutsche ndesbank-rozentrale 5.67)	Credito Italiano S.p.A. (16.67)	National Westminster Bank Ltd. (16.67)	Chase Manhattan Overseas Banking Corporation (16.67)	Royal Bank of Canada (16.67); Mitsubishi Bank Ltd. (16.67)
yerische reinsbank ;				Schweizerische Bankengesellschaft (55);

Year of establishment	Name	Head office	Capital	France
1971				
	Eurodeal Ltd.	London		
	Nordic Bank Ltd.	London		
	Centrofin	Wien	7 Mill. öS	Banque Occidentale pour l'Industrie et le Commerce (14.3)
	International Mergers Service AG	Zürich/ London	0.150 Mill. sfrs[6]	

Participating banks (with % held)				
ermany	*Italy*	*Britain*	*USA*	*Other countries*
erliner Bank '); ereinsbank Hamburg ')				Dow Banking Corporation, Zürich (10); Lavoro Bank AG, Zürich (7); Intersoge S.A., Zürich (7)
al. Oppeneim jr. & ie.		Western American Bank[5]; Hambros Bank		
				Den norske Creditbank (33.33); Kansallis-Osake-Pankki (33.33); Svenska Handelsbanken (33.33)
	Banco di Sicilia (14.3)	Kleinwort, Benson Ltd. (14.3)		Banco Popular Español, Madrid (14.3); Bank of Tokyo Ltd. (14.3); Bank für Arbeit und Wirtschaft, Wien (14.3); Bank Handlowy w Warzawie S.A., Warschau (14.3)
Aufhäuser	Banca Nazionale dell' Agricoltura	Singer & Friedlaender Ltd.	Booz, Allen & Hamilton Inc.	N.V. Slavenburgs Bank; Banque du Benelux; Société Nationale d'Investissement; R. Henriques jr., Kopenhagen; Allied Irish Investment Bank Ltd., Dublin; Schoeller & Co., Wien; Banco Totta & Acores, Lissabon;

97

Year of establishment	Name	Head office	Capital	France
1971				
	Bank of America Ltd.	London	10 Mill. £	
	UBS-DB Corporation[8]	New York	0.080 Mill. US-$	
	Banque of Ameribas S.A.	Luxembourg	1,200 Mill. bfrs	Banque de Paris et des Pays-Bas (40)
1972	European Brazilian Bank Ltd., "EUROBRAZ"	London	4 Mill. £	
	Merril Lynch-Brown Shipley Bank Ltd.	London		
	UBAF Ltd.	London	5 Mill. £	Union de Banques Arabes et Francaises (50)
	Associated Banks of Europe Corporation, "ABECOR"	Brüssel	10 Mill. bfrs	Banque National de Paris

	Participating banks (with % held)			
ermany	*Italy*	*Britain*	*USA*	*Other countries*
				Banco de Santander, Madrid; Barif, Madrid
		Kleinwort, Benson Ltd. (25)	Bank of America (75)	
eutsche Bank G (50)				Schweizerische Bankgesellschaft (50)
			Bank of America (60)	
eutsche Bank G (13.5)			Bank of America International Ltd. (16)	Banco do Brazil (32); Bank of America International S.A., Luxembourg (16); Schweizerische Bankgesellschaft (13.5); Dai-Ichi Kangyo Bank (9)
		Brown Shipley Holdings Ltd. (26)	Merril Lynch Holdings Ltd. (74)	
		Midland Bank Ltd. (25)		Libyan Arab Foreign Bank (25)
resdner Bank G; ayerische Hytheken- und echselbank	Banca Nazionale del Lavoro	Barclays Bank Ltd.		Algemene Bank Nederland N.V.; Banque de Bruxelles S.A.; Banque Internationale à Luxembourg; Österreichische Länderbank

99

Year of estab-lishment	Name	Head office	Capital	France
1972	A.B.D. Securities Corporation	New York/ Boston	5 Mill. US-$	
	Libra Bank	London	6.3 Mill. £	
1973	U.B.A.E. Union de Banques Arabes et Européennes S.A.	Luxembourg	30 Mill. DM	Union de Banques Arabes et Françaises, U.B.A.F. (33.33)
	Orion Leasing Hold-ings Ltd.	London	1.98 Mill. £	
	Multinational Orion Leasing Hold-ings N.V.	Amsterdam	78 Mill. hfl	
	Orion Pacific Ltd.	Hong Kong	62.5 Mill. HK $	

	Participating banks (with % held)			

rmany	Italy	Britain	USA	Other countries
esdner Bank); yerische Hy- theken- und :chselbank)				Algemene Bank Nederland N.V. (25); Banque de Bruxelles S.A. (25)
stdeutsche ndesbank- ozentrale .6)	Credito Italiano S.p.A. (7.1)	National Westminster Bank Ltd. (5)	Chase Manhattan Overseas Banking Corporation (23.6)	Royal Bank of Canada (10.6); Mitsubishi Bank Ltd. (10.6); Swiss Bank Corporation (10.6); Banco Espirito Santo e Commercial de Lisboa (5.9); Banco Itau (8); Banco de Comercio (8)
mmerzbank ; Bayerische einsbank; stdeutsche ndesbank- ozentrale gether 33.33)				Arab Bank Ltd.; Arab Bank (Overseas) Ltd. (together 33.33)
stdeutsche ndesbank- ozentrale .67)	Credito Italiano S.p.A. (16.67)	National Westminster Bank Ltd. (16.67)	Chase Manhattan Overseas Banking Corporation (16.67)	Royal Bank of Canada (16.67); Mitsubishi Bank Ltd. (16.67)
stdeutsche ndesbank- ozentrale .67)	Credito Italiano S.p.A. (16.67)	National Westminster Bank Ltd. (16.67)	Chase Manhattan Overseas Banking Corporation (16.67)	Royal Bank of Canada (16.67); Mitsubishi Bank Ltd. (16.67)
stdeutsche ndesbank- ozentrale)	Credito Italiano S.p.A.	National Westminster Bank Ltd. (15)	Chase Manhattan Overseas Banking Corporation	Royal Bank of Canada; Mitsubishi Bank Ltd; Nikko Securities Company

Year of estab-lishment	Name	Head office	Capital	France
1973	European Banking Company Ltd.	London	10.0 Mill. £	
	Anglo-Romanian Bank Ltd.	London		
	Hungarian International Bank	London		
	International Energy Bank Ltd.	London		Banque de la Société Financière Européenne (20); Banque Worms (10)
	Iran Overseas Investment Bank	London	5.0 Mill. £	Société Générale (10)
	London & Continental Bankers Ltd.	London		Banque Féderative du Crédit Mutuel (2.51);

		Participating banks (with % held)		
Germany	Italy	Britain	USA	Other countries
Deutsche Bank AG (14.3)	Banca Commerciale Italiana	Midland Bank Ltd. (14.3)		Amsterdam-Rotterdam Bank (14.3); Creditanstalt-Bankverein (14.3); Société Générale de Banque (14.3); Société Générale (14.3)
		Barclays Bank (30)	Manufacturers Hanover International (20)	Romanian Bank for Foreign Trade (50)
				National Bank of Hungary (60); Hungarian Foreign Trade Bank (15); National Savings Bank/Hungary (15); Centrale Wechsel- und Creditbank (10)
		Bank of Scotland (15); Barclays Bank International (15)	Republic National Bank of Dallas (20)	Canadian Imperial Bank of Commerce (20)
Deutsche Bank 0)		Barclays Bank International (10); Manufacturers Hanover International (10); Midland Bank (10)	Bank of America (10)	Bank Melli Iran (10); Bank of Tokyo (10); Industrial Bank of Japan (10); Industrial and Mining Development Bank of Iran (10)
eutsche enossenhaftskasse 0.24)	Banca Nazionale dell'Agricoltura (2.51)	S.G. Warburg & Co. Ltd. (4.55)		Centrale Rabobank Netherlands (10.05);

Year of estab-lishment	Name	Head office	Capital	France
1973				Caisse Natio-nale de Crédit Agricole (7.54)
1974	Euro-Latinamerican Bank	London	12 Mill. £	Banque Natio-nale de Paris (5)
	International Mexican Bank	London	5.0 Mill. £	Paribas Inter-national (7.25)

Participating banks (with % held)				
Germany	Italy	Britain	USA	Other countries
				Genossen-schaftliche Zentralbank Austria (10.05); Andelsbanken AmbA, Denmark (5.02); Osuuspankkien Keskuspankki Oy, Finland (2.51); Jordbrukets Bank, Sweden (2.51); Raiffeizenkas van de Belgische Boerenbond (2.51)
Dresdner Bank (5); Bayerische Hypotheken- und Wechselbank (5); Deutsch-Südamerikanische Bank (2)	Banca Nazionale del Lavoro (5)	Barclays Bank International (5)		Banco do Brasil (6); Banco de Colombia (6); Banco de Londres y Mexico (6); Banco de la Nación Perú (6); Algemene Bank Nederland (5); Banque de Bruxelles (5); Österreichische Länderbank (5); Banco Mercantil de Sao Paulo (1); Banco Central (Spain) (5)
Deutsche Bank (7.25)			Bank of America International Ltd. (20)	Banco Nacional de Mexico (38); Inlat, S.A. de C.V. (Grupo Senderos), Mexico (13); Dai-Ichi Kangyo Bank (7.25); Schweizerische Bankgesellschaft (7.25)

Notes

1. In 1973 the name was changed from Banque Européenne de Crédit à Moyen Terme to Banque Européenne de Crédit.

2. The EABC was formed in 1968 out of the Belgian American Banking Corporation (founded 1950) whose shareholders until then were the Société Générale de Banque and its affiliated companies.

3. The EABTS was formed in 1968 out of the Belgian-American Bank & Trust Company (founded 1952) whose shareholders until then were the Société Générale de Banque and its affiliated companies.

4. Banks of the Five Arrows Group have an interest of 45.470 per cent in total.

5. Majority stake.

6. Up to now 120,000 sfrs of the capital has been taken over by 13 institutions.

7. Orion Termbank took over the share capital of Orion Bank Ltd. and changed its name to Orion Bank Ltd. The merger became effective on December 30, 1974.

8. The UBS-DB Corp. was formed out of the American UBS Corp. (founded in 1970 as a wholly owned subsidiary of the Schweizerische Bankgesellschaft).

Sources

Jürgen Stein: Multinationale Banken werden immer vielseitiger, in *Bank-Betrieb*, Vol. 12 (1972) No. 4, p. 152 ff.; Alberto Ferrari: New ways of international cooperation in banking, in *Banking in a Changing World*, Lectures and Proceedings at the 24th International Banking Summer School held at Chianciano, Rome, May 1971, p. 88 ff.; The Banker Research Unit (Publ.): *Who owns what in world banking 1973-74*, London, September 1973; and the company files of the HWWA Institute.

APPENDIX 2

Principal subsidiary and affiliated interests of major American banks abroad

Name	Percentage held

Bankamerica Corporation
(one bank holding company for the Bank of America N.T.
and S.A.)

Ameribas Holding S.A.,[2] Luxembourg	60%
Amparis B.V.,[2] Amsterdam	50%
Banca d'America e d'Italia, Milan	97%
Banco Comercial para America,[1] Madrid	50%
Banco Intercontinental Espanol,[1] Madrid	25%
Bank of America International S.A., Luxembourg	58%
Bank of America (Guernsey) Ltd.,[2] Guernsey	100%
Bank of America (Jersey) Ltd.,[1] Jersey	100%
Bank of America S.A.,[1] Luxembourg	100%
Bank of Credit & Commerce International S.A.,[1] Luxembourg	43%
Bank America Finance Ltd.,[2] Reading/K.K.	100%
Bank America Williams Glyn Factors Ltd.,[2] London	51%
Bankhaus Centrale Credit AG,[2] Düsseldorf	100%
Banque de la Société Financière Européenne,[2] Paris	6%
BBA Leasing S.A.,[2] Madrid	50%
Cegebail,[2] Lille	25%
Corner Banca S.A.,[1] Lugano	20%
European Brazilian Bank Ltd.,[1] London	35%
The Hellenic Bank Ltd.,[1] Nicosia/Cyprus	20%
Interfinanciera, S.A.,[1] Madrid	10%
International Mexican Bank Ltd.,[1] London	20%
International Nuclear Credit Corporation,[1] Paris	11%
Interpromotora S.A.,[1] Madrid	15%
Investment Bank Ltd.,[1] Athens	20%
Iran Overseas Investment Bank Ltd.,[1] London	10%
Rabomerica International Bank N.V.,[1] Amsterdam	50%
Société Financière pour les pays d'Outre-Mer,[1] Geneva	25%
Société Financière Européenne,[2] Luxembourg	12%
Turkish Foreign Trade Bank,[1] Istanbul	20%
Wobaco Holding Ltd.,[1] Luxembourg	48%
Société de Coopération Industrielle Franco-Soviétique,[2] Moscow	25%

Name	Percentage held

Citicorporation
(holding company for First National City Bank, New York)

Citicorp. Data Services, Switzerland	–
Citicorp. International Bank Ltd., London	–
Cofinance S.A., Switzerland	100%
Computer Projects Ltd., U.K.	–
Credit S.A., Belgium	59%
Fimen S.A., Belgium	100%
Financia S.A., Belgium	100%
First National City Bank (Belgium) S.A.	100%
First National City Bank (Channel Islands) Ltd., Luxembourg	100%
First National City Bank (Luxembourg) S.A.	100%
FNCB Eurosecurities S.A., Belgium	100%
Hypotheek- en Beheermaatschappij Financia N.V., Belgium	84%
National City Financial Trust Ltd., U.K.	100%
Banco de Financiacion Industrial, Spain	5%
Banque Internationale pour l'Afrique Occidentale, France	49%
Citicorp. International Securities S.A., Belgium	–
First National City Flaminia – Holding di Servizi Finanziari S.p.A., Italy	50%
Interbank AG, Austria	50%
National & Grindlays Bank Ltd., U.K.	40%
Securities Management Company Ltd., Luxembourg	25%

The Chase Manhattan Corporation
(holding company for the Chase Manhattan Bank N.A.)

Chase Manhattan Bank (Austria) AG, Vienna	74.5%
Chase Manhattan Bank Luxembourg S.A., Luxembourg	–
Chase Manhattan Bank (Switzerland), Geneva	100%
Chase Manhattan Bank Trust Corp. Ltd., London	100%
Chase Manhattan Ltd., London	–
Chase Manhattan S.A., Paris	–
Financière d'Investissements et de	

Name	*Percentage held*
Construction Immobilière, Paris	–
Union Immobilière Internationale S.A., Paris	–
Banque de Commerce S.A., Antwerp	–
Capital International S.A., Geneva	50%
Chase Bank of Ireland International Ltd., Dublin	50%
Equipement Leasing Co. Ltd., London	–
Familienbank AG, West Germany	–
Libra Bank Ltd., London	–
National Investment Bank for Industrial Development, Athens	–
Nederlandse Credietbank N.V., Amsterdam	–
Orion Bank Ltd., London	–
Orion Multinational Services Ltd., London	–
Orion Leasing Holdings Ltd., London	–
Multinational Orion Leasing Holdings N.V., Amsterdam	–
Standard & Chase Bank C.I. Ltd., Channel Islands	–
Standard & Chase Trust Co. C.I. Ltd., Channel Islands	–
Standard & Chartered Banking Group Ltd., London	–
Banque de Réescompte et de Placement (B.A.R.E.P.)	–
Liga Financiera S.A., Spain	–
Transleasing S.A., Spain	–

J. P. Morgan & Co. Inc.
(holding company for Morgan Guaranty Trust Company)

Banca Morgan Vonwiller S.p.A., Rome	51%
First Arts Leasing Company S.A., Brussels	100%
Morgan & Cie. S.A., Paris (holds 33% of Morgan & Cie. International S.A., Paris)	61%
Morgan Guaranty Finance Ltd., Hamilton	100%
Morgan Guaranty Investment Services S.A., Geneva	100%
Banco del Desarollo Economico Espanol S.A., Madrid	4%
Caisse de Gestion Mobilière, Paris	10%

Name	Percentage held
Epargne Interessement, Paris	23%
Euro-clear Clearance System Ltd., London	3%
European Enterprises Development G.S.A., Luxembourg	6%
H.F.C. Trust Ltd., London	25%
Mees & Hope Group N.K., Amsterdam	20%
Morgan Grenfell Holdings Ltd., London	32%
Neue Bank AG, Zurich	10%
Ste. Holding de Financement et de Crédit, Basle	less than 1%
Ste. Nationale d'Investissement, Brussels	less than 1%

Bankers Trust New York Corporation
(holding company for Bankers Trust Company)

Bankers Trust, Zurich	100%
Bankers Trust Factors Ltd., London	56%
Bankers Trust Financiaria, Rome	100%
Bankers Trust International Ltd., London	100%
Deutsche Unionbank GmbH, Frankfurt	68%
Banque du Benelux S.A., Brussels	33.33%

Chemical New York Corporation
(holding company for Chemical Bank)

Chemical Bank Trustee Company Ltd., London	100%
Chembank Nominees Ltd., London	100%
London Multinational Bank, London	30%
Breisach Pinschaf Schoeller, Vienna	25%

Continental Illinois Corporation
(bank holding company for Continental Illinois Bank & Trust Company of Chicago)

Conill Bank AG, Vienna	–
Continental Bank S.A./N.V., Brussels	–
Continental Illinois Bank (Switzerland), Zurich	–
Continental Illinois Ltd., London	–
Continental International Finance, Luxembourg	–

Name	Percentage held
Adela Investment Co. S.A., Luxembourg	–
Banca di Messina, Messina	–
Banca Privata Finanziara, Milan	25%
Banco Atlantico, Madrid	–
Banco Crefisul de Investimento S.A., Port Allegre	–
Banque de Financement S.A., Geneva	–
Crédit Commercial de France, Paris	–
Greyhound Financial & Leasing Corporation A.G., Zug/Switzerland	–
H & H Factors Ltd., London	–
Leasing Italiana S.p.A., Milan	–
Union Industrial Bancaria, Barcelona	–
Lease and Industrial Finance Co. Ltd., Brisbane	–

First Chicago Corporation
(holding company of First National Bank of Chicago)

First Chicago Holding (U.K.) Ltd., U.K.	100%
First Chicago Investments (U.K.) Ltd., U.K.	100%
First Chicago Leasing (U.K.) Ltd., U.K.	100%
First Chicago Ltd., U.K.	100%
First Chicago Nominees Ltd., U.K.	100%
First Chicago Nominees (Ireland) Ltd., Ireland	100%
First Chicago Overseas Finance, N.V.	100%
First Chicago Services Ltd.	100%
N.V. Slavenburg's Bank, The Netherlands	20%
Commercial Bank of Wales, U.K.	20%
International Commercial Bank, London	22%
Starwood Associates, U.K.	46.5%

First National Boston Corporation
(holding company for the First National Bank of Boston)

Bank of Boston S.A., Luxembourg	100%
Boston Investment and Financial Services S.A., Geneva	100%
Boston Leasing GmbH, Frankfurt	100%
Boston Overseas Holdings, S.A., Luxembourg	100%
Boston Trust & Savings Ltd., Frankfurt	100%
First National Boston Ltd., London	100%

Name	Percentage held
International Factoring and Leasing AG, Zug/Switzerland	100%
Old Colony Nominees Ltd., London	100%
Banco Europeo de Negocios, Madrid	2%
Factors AG, Zurich	100%
Inter-Factor Bank AG, Mainz	10%
International Factors Austria GmbH, Vienna	25%
International Factors Belgium S.A., Brussels	33%
International Factors France, Paris	15%
International Factors Ltd., Copenhagen	–
International Factors (Ireland) Ltd., Dublin	–
International Factors Italia S.p.A., Milan	7%
International Factors Nederland N.V., Rotterdam	25%
International Factors (Portugal) SARL, Lisbon	20%
International Factors Espanola S.A., Madrid	23%
International Factors AB, Stockholm	10%
International Factors Ltd., Brighton U.K.	25%
Suomen Interfactors Oy, Helsinki	10%

Manufacturers Hanover Corporation
(holding company for the Manufacturers Hanover Trust Company)

Commercial Export Credit Co. Ltd., London	100%
Manufacturers Hanover Bank/Belgium, Brussels	98%
Manufacturers Hanover Banque Nordique, Paris	60%
Manufacturers Hanover Ltd., London	75%
Manufacturers Hanover Executor & Trustee Co. Ltd., London	100%
Ocean Acceptances (London) Ltd.	–
Ocean Finance and Trust Corporation Ltd., Guernsey	–
Iran Overseas Investment Bank Ltd., London	–

Marine Midland Banks Inc.
(holding company for ten full service banks which operate throughout New York State)

Marine Midland Overseas GmbH, Germany	100%
Marinvest S.A., Luxembourg	100%

Name	Percentage held
Banque de l'Union Européenne S.A., France	19.09%
Uluslararasi Endustrie Ve Ticaret Bankasi A.S., Turkey	24%
Interunion-Banque S.A., France	19.40%
Sitalfin S.p.A., Italy	24.90%
Union Auxiliaire de Financement 'UNIMAR', France	50%
Irish Intercontinental Bank Ltd., Ireland	30.66%

Mellon National Corporation
(bank holding company for Mellon Bank N.A.)

Eurofinance, Paris	–
First Boston (Europe) Ltd., London	33%

Security Pacific National Bank

Western American Bank (Europe) Ltd., London	22.5%

Wells Fargo & Co.
(holding company for Wells Fargo Bank N.A., San Francisco)

Wells Fargo Ltd., London	100%
Allgemeine Deutsche Credit-Anstalt (ADCA)	25%
Crédit Chimique, Paris	15%
Western American Bank (Europe) Ltd., London	22%

Western Bancorporation
(holding company for 23 banks in the 11 western states)

United California Bank S.A./N.V., Brussels	–
Financiera de California, Madrid	50%

Name	Percentage held
Bankamerica Corporation	
Montreal Trust Co.,[1] Montreal	20%
North Continent Capital Ltd., Vancouver	49%
Citicorporation	
FNCB Capital Canada Ltd.	100%
International Trust Company, Canada	100%
The Mercantile Bank of Canada	100%
The Chase Manhattan Corporation	
Arcturus Investment & Development Ltd., Montreal	–
CMB Holdings Ltd., Toronto	–
J.P. Morgan & Co. Inc.	
J.P. Morgan of Canada Ltd., Toronto	100%
Continental Illinois Corporation	
Builders Financial Co. Ltd., Toronto	–
First Chicago Corporation	
Canadian Real Estate Research Corporation	24,8%
First Chicago Leasing of Canada Ltd.	100%
Marine Midland Banks Inc.	
Roy Marine Leasing Co. Ltd., Canada	75%

Name	Percentage held

Bankamerica Corporation

Name	Percentage held
ADELA Investment U.S.A., Lima	1%
Arrendadora Comermex S.A. de C.V.,[2] Mexico City	44%
Bamerical Mortgage & Finance Co.,[2] San Jose/ Puerto Rico	100%
Banco Internacional S.A.,[1] Rio de Janeiro	50%
Bank of America New York,[1] Nassau/Bahamas	100%
Bank of America S.A.,[1] San Jose/Bahamas	100%
Corporación Financiera Asociada S.A.,[2] Santo Domingo	20%
Corporación Financiera S.A.,[1] Mexico City	20%
Financiera de America S.A.,[2] San Jose/Costa Rica	51%
Financiera Americana Ltda.,[1] Santiago/Chile	95%
Financiera Bamerical S.A.,[2] Panama City	100%
Jamaican American Merchant Bankers Ltd.,[2] Kingston	100%
Latin American Agribusiness Development Corp.,[2] Panama City	8%
Metro America C.A.,[2] Caracas	40%
Handels Industrial and Credit Bank N.V.,[1] Surinam	10%

Citicorporation

Name	Percentage held
Banco Argentino del Atlantic, Argentina	80%
Banco de Honduras S.A.	96%
Citybank Credito, Financiamento e Investimento S.A., Brazil	100%
Compañia Colombiana de Financiamentos S.A., Colombia	100%
Financiera Intercomercial S.A., Panama	100%
First National City (Costa Rica) S.A.	100%
First National City Trust Company (Bahamas) Ltd.	100%
First National Finance Ltd., Jamaica	100%
Inversiones Citycol S.A., Colombia	–
Inversiones y Adelantos C.A., Venezuela	100%
Ripco S.A. C.I. y F., Argentina	–
Banco de Caldes, Colombia	20%

Name	Percentage held
Banco de Investimento Industrial S.A., Brazil	17%
Caribbean Merchant Bank Ltd., Jamaica	–
Compañia de Turismo Promocoes e Administracao, Brazil	–
Corporación Financiera de Occidente, Colombia	17%
Prestarmo Presto, Puerto Rico	–

The Chase Manhattan Corporation

Name	Percentage held
Atlantic Bank Ltd., Belize	–
Banco de Investimento Lar Brasileiro, Rio de Janeiro	–
Banco Lar Brasileiro S.A., Rio de Janeiro	–
Financeiro Lar Brasileiro S.A., Rio de Janeiro	–
Chase Manhattan Trust Cayman Ltd., Cayman Islands	–
Chase Manhattan Costa Rica S.A., San Jose	–
Chase Merchant Bankers Jamaica Ltd., Kingston	–
Housing Investment Corporation Puerto Rico, San Juan	–
Banco Atlantida S.A., Honduras	
The Chase Manhattan Trust Corporation Ltd., Nassau	100%
Banco Argentino de Comercio, Buenos Aires	–
Banco del Comercio, Bogota	–
Banco Mercantil y Agricola C.A., Caracas	–
Costa Rican Farms S.A., San Jose	–
Desarrollo Agropecuario del Disquis S.A., San Jose	–
Estalsa S.A., La Paz	–
Peruinvest – Compañia de Fomento e Inversiones S.A., Lima	–
Société Antillaise de Produits Chimiques, Martinique	–
Textilera Tres Rios S.A., San Jose	–
International Americas Finance Inc., Panama	–
Arrendacima C.A., Venezuela	–
Consorcio Inversionista Mercantil y Agricola C.A., Venezuela	–

Name	Percentage held

J.P. Morgan & Co. Inc.

Morgan Servicos e Participacoes Limitada, São Paulo	100%
Banco Finasa de Investimento S.A., São Paulo	13%
Banco Frances del Rio de la Plata S.A., Buenos Aires	44%
Financiera Banamex S.A., Mexico City	5%
Industrias Reconquista S.A., Buenos Aires	10%
Peruinvest — Compañia de Fomento e Inversiones S.A., Lima	14%

Chemical New York Corporation

Chemical Overseas Finance Corporation, Panama	100%
Productora de Articulos de Celuosa Keys S.A. de CV, Mexico	100%
Sociedad Financiera Exterior S.A.	30%
Bank of New Providence, Nassau	50%

Bankers Trust New York Corporation

Bullrich S.A. de Inversiones, Buenos Aires	20%
Corporacion Financiera Nacional, Colombia	6.7%

Continental Illinois Corporation

Continental Assessoria Financeira e Servicos Ltda., São Paulo	–
Banco Shaw S.A., Buenos Aires	–
Caribbean Bank, Cayman Islands	–
Compania Financiera Ecuabriana de Desarrollo S.A. (COFIEC, S.A.), Quito/Ecuador	–
Corporacion Financiera del Valle, Cali/ Colombia	–
Crown Continental Merchant Bank Jamaica Ltd., Kingston/Jamaica	–

First Chicago Corporation

Arrendadores e Inversionistas Latina	100%

Name	Percentage held
First Chicago (Costa Rica) S.A.	100%
First Chicago Merchant Bank (Jamaica) Ltd.	100%
The First National Bank of Chicago (Jamaica) Ltd.	100%
Maja S.R.L.	100%

First National Boston Corporation

Bank of Boston Trust Company (Bahamas) Ltd., Nassau	100%
Boston Distribuidora de Titulos e Valores Mobilarios Ltda., São Paulo	100%
Boston Financeira S.A., São Paulo	100%
Boston Leasing-Arrendamento, Representacoes e Servicios, Ltda., São Paulo	100%
Boston S.A., Administracas cie Empreenderientos, São Paulo	100%
Caribbean American Service Investment and Finance Co., Ltd., Grand Cayman	100%
Corporacion Financiera de Boston, Buenos Aires	100%
International Factors S.A., Buenos Aires	100%
Sociedad Anonima de Servicios e Universiones, Buenos Aires	100%
Arrendadora Industrial Venezolana C.A., Caracas	24%
Arrendadora Industrial S.A., Mexico City	40%
Compania de Credito S.A., San Pedro Sula/Honduras	50%
Corporacion Internacional de Boston S.A., San Jose/Costa Rica	50%
Servicios Commerciales e Industriales S.A., Guatemala City	50%

Manufacturers Hanover Corporation

MHT—Servicos e Administracao Ltd., São Paulo	100%

Marine Midland Banks Inc.

Intermarine do Brazil Ltda., Brazil	100%

Name	Percentage held
Sociedad Financiera Union C.A., Venezuela	40%
Marmid Finance Ltd., Venezuela	100%
Almacenadora S.A., Costa Rica	22%
Arawak Trust Company Ltd., Bahamas	10.7%
Arawak Trust Company (Cayman) Ltd., Cayman Islands	11%
Corporacion Financiera del Norte, Colombia	20%
Crece S.A., Costa Rica	20%
Ficentro S.A., Panama	22.4%

Mellon National Corporation

Banco Bozano, Simonzen de Investimento S.A., Rio de Janeiro	25%

Security Pacific National Bank

Security Pacific Administracao e Services Ltd., São Paulo	99%

Wells Fargo & Co.

Corporation Interamerica S.A., Mexico City	20%
Empress Financieras Continental, Panama	25%
Financiera de Desarrollo e Inversion S.A., El Salvador	14%
Financiera Nacional S.A., Caracas	40%
Interamericana de Arrendamientos S.A., Mexico City	21%
Banco de America, Nicaragua	19%

Western Bancorporation

Corporacion Nicaraguense de Inversiones, Managua/Nicaragua	20.3%

Name	Percentage held

Bankamerica Corporation

Name	Percentage held
Bank of America (Maroc) Ltd.,[1] Casablanca	100%
Bank of America (Nigeria) Ltd.,[1] Lagos	100%
Commercial Bank of Malawi,[2] Blantyre	30%
National Bank of Oman,[1] Muscat	20%

Citicorporation

Name	Percentage held
First National City Bank (Maghreb), Marocco	100%
First National City Bank (South Africa) Ltd.	100%
First National City Bank (Zaire) S.A.R.L.	100%
First National City Bank of New York (Nigeria) Ltd.	100%
New York London Trustee Co. Ltd., Liberia	100%
The Bank of Monrovia, Liberia	100%

The Chase Manhattan Corporation

Name	Percentage held
African Ponderose Ltd., Mombasa	–
Banque Ivoirienne de Développement Industriel, Abidjan	–
Commercial Bank of Dubai Ltd., Dubai	–
Nigerian Industrial Development Bank Ltd., Lagos	–
Standard Bank of West Africa Ltd., Gambia	–
Standard Bank Ghana Ltd.	–
Standard Bank Ltd., Lesotho	–
National Bank of Malawi	–
Standard Bank Nigeria Ltd.	–
Standard Bank Sierra Leone Ltd.	–
The Standard Bank of South Africa Ltd.	–
The Standard Bank Swaziland Ltd.	–
Standard Bank Uganda Ltd.	–
Standard Bank Zambia Ltd.	–

J.P. Morgan & Co. Inc.

Name	Percentage held
Bank Almashrek S.A.L., Beyrouth	40%
Banque Commerciale Congolaise, Brazzaville	4%
Banque Commerciale Zairoise, Kinshasa	4%

121

Name	Percentage held
Banque de Kigali, Ruanda	10%
Banque Nationale pour le Développement Economique, Rabat/Marocco	2%
National Investment Bank, Accra/Ghana	1%
Ste. Camerounaise de Banque, Yaounde	5%
Ste. Financière de Développement, Kinshasa	3%
Ste. Ivoirienne de Banque, Abidjan	12%
Union Bancaire pour le Commerce et l'Industrie, Tunis	6%
Union Gabonaise de Banque, Libreville	15%
Union Sénégalaise de Banque pour le Commerce et l'Industrie, Dakar	4%

Chemical New York Corporation

Northwest Iron Company Ltd., Tasmania	10%
Bank of Liberia, Monrovia	47.6%

Bankers Trust New York Corporation

Société Générale de Banques au Cameroun, Yaounde	10%
Société Générale de Banques au Congo, Brazzaville	10%
Société Générale au Côte d'Ivoire, Abidjan	10%
Société Générale de Banques au Sénégal, Dakar	10%
United Bank for Africa Ltd., Lagos	6.67%

Continental Illinois Corporation

Continental Development Bank SAL, Beirut	–
Banque Americano-Franco-Suisse pour le Maroc, Casablanca	–
Industrial & Mining Development Bank of Iran, Teheran	–
Commercial Bank Zambia Ltd., Lusaka	–

First National Boston Corporation

International Factors (South Africa) Ltd.,

Name	Percentage held
Johannesburg	10%
International Factors (Israel) Ltd., Tel Aviv	10%
Wells Fargo & Co.	
Dubai Bank Ltd., Dubai	10%
Western Bancorporation	
Banque du Crédit Populaire, Beyrouth	41.3%

Name	Percentage held

Bankamerica Corporation

Agricultural Finance Corporation,[1] Bombay	1%
Asian & Euro-American Capital Corp. Ltd.,[2] Hong Kong	30%
Asian & Euro-American Merchant Bank Ltd.,[2] Singapore	30%
Asian & Euro-American Merchant Bankers (Malaysia) Berhad,[2] Kuala Lumpur	23%
Asian & Euro-American Capital Corp. (Thailand) Ltd.,[2] Bangkok	30%
BA Finance (Hong Kong) Ltd.,[2] Hong Kong	100%
BA Finance Corp. of the Philippines,[2] Makati	40%
BA Leasing and Capital (Hong Kong) Ltd.,[2] Hong Kong	75%
Bamerical Financial Corp. Ltd.,[2] Bangkok	100%
Foreign Trade Bank of Iran,[1] Teheran	16%
General Lease Co. Ltd., Osaka	–
The Inzular Bank of Asia and America,[1] Manila	30%
Iran-California Co. Inc.,[2] Teheran	19%
Tokyo Investment Services (International) Inc.,[1] Tokyo	50%

Citicorporation

Asian Pacific Capital Corporation Ltd., Hong Kong	–
Citicorp Credit, Guam	–
Citicorp Financial Ltd., Singapore	–
Far East Bank Ltd., Hong Kong	76%
FNCB Finance Inc., Philippines	75%
FNCB Financial Ltd., Hong Kong	100%
International Data Systems Service Ltd., Hong Kong	100%
Rakyat First Merchant Bankers, Kuala Lumpur	45%
CCP Securities Corp., Philippines	–
Bangkok First Investment & Trust Ltd.	50%
Commercial Credit Corporation (Thailand) Ltd.	39%
Feati Bank, Manila	40%
First National City Development Finance Corp. (Thailand)	100%

Name	*Percentage held*
First National Nippon Shimpan Co. Ltd., Japan	40%
First Overseas Credit Ltd., Singapore	40%
Fuji National City Consulting Ltd., Japan	50%
Fuyo General Lease Co. Ltd., Japan	20%
Iranians' Bank, Iran	35%
Taiwan First Investment Trust Co. Ltd.	50%

The Chase Manhattan Corporation

Chase Manhattan Investment Co. (Thailand) Ltd., Bangkok	–
Kam Yuan Choy Mo, Hong Kong	–
Credit & Development Corporation, Manila	–
Diamond Lease Company Ltd., Tokyo	–
Filinvest Credit Corporation, Manila	–
International Agrobusiness Corporation of Iran, Teheran	–
International Discount Co., Singapore	10%
Mah-In Industries Inc., Seoul	–
Mitsubishi Chase Manhattan Consulting Co., Tokyo	–
Commercial Bank & Trust Company of the Philippines, Manila	30%
Philippine American Investment Corporation, Philippines	20%
United Chase Merchant Bankers Ltd., Singapore	–
Orion Pacific Ltd., Hong Kong	–
Diamond Lease (Hong Kong) Ltd., Hong Kong	–

J.P. Morgan & Co. Inc.

Bank of the Philippines Islands, Manila	20%
China Development Corporation, Taipei	10%
Industrial Credit & Investment Corp. of India, Bombay	less than 1%
Malaysian Industrial Development Berhard, Kuala Lumpur	less than 1%
Morgan Guaranty & Partners Ltd., Singapore	40%
National Discount Company Ltd., Singapore	35%
Pakistan Industrial Credit and Investment	

Name	Percentage held
Corp. Ltd., Karachi	1%
P.T. Merchant Investment Corporation, Jakarta	36%

Bankers Trust New York Corporation

BT Finance Ltd., Hong Kong	–
Thai Investment & Securities Co. Ltd., Bangkok	67%
Korea Invest. Finance Company, Seoul	–

Continental Illinois Corporation

Continental Illinois (HK) Ltd., Hong Kong	–
Continental Illinois Thailand Ltd., Bangkok	–
China Investment and Trust Co., Taipei	–
House of Investments Inc., Manila	–
Malaysian International Merchant Bankers Berhad, Kuala Lumpur	–
Pakistan Industrial Credit Investment, Karachi	–
Private Development Corporation of the Philippines, Manila	–
Private Investment Co. for Asia (PICA) S.A., Tokyo	–
Singapore International Merchant Bankers Ltd., Singapore	–

First Chicago Corporation

First Chicago Hong Kong Ltd., Hong Kong	100%
First Chicago Nominees Pte. Ltd., Hong Kong	100%
First Chicago (Singapore) Pte., Ltd., Singapore	100%
The First National Bank of Chicago (Lebanon) S.A.L., Beirut	100%

First National Boston Corporation

First National Boston (Hong Kong) Ltd., Hong Kong	100%
Orient Factors Ltd., Tokyo	10%

Name	Percentage held
Pacific Lease Company Ltd., Tokyo	10%
Manufacturers Hanover Corporation	
Manufacturers Hanover (Asia)Ltd., Hong Kong	–
Financial Corporation of Indonesia, Jakarta	–
Marine Midland Banks Inc.	
Marine Midland (Thailand) Ltd., Thailand	100%
Central Lease Company Ltd., Japan	9.9%
Malaysia Industrial Finance Corp. Berhad, Malaysia	15%
Mellon National Corporation	
Development and Investment Bank of Iran, Teheran	–
Wells Fargo & Co.	
Shanghai Commercial Bank Ltd., Hong Kong	20%
WMS Capital Corporation, Hong Kong	40%
Western Bancorporation	
Western International Capital Ltd., Hong Kong	–

Name	Percentage held

Bankamerica Corporation

Banque de Paris et des Pays-Bas Nouvelle Caledonie,[1] Noumea	30%
Commercial and General Acceptance Ltd.,[2] Sydney	20%
Lease Underwriting Pty. Ltd., Sydney	20%
MBC International Ltd.,[2] Melbourne	25%
New Zealand United Corporation Ltd.,[2] Wellington	20%
Pacific International Trust Co. Ltd.,[2] Vila	20%
Partnership Pacific Ltd.,[2] Sydney	33%

Citicorporation

Citi National (Holdings) Pty. Ltd.	45%
FNCB-Waltons Corporation Ltd.	50%
Industrial Acceptance Corporation Ltd.	33%
PFCB Ltd.	20%

The Chase Manhattan Corporation

Alliance Acceptance Co. Ltd., Australia	–
All-States Commercial Bills Ltd., Melbourne	–
Alliance Holdings Ltd., Sydney	33.3%
Chase-N.B.A. Group Depository Ltd., Melbourne	–
Chase-N.B.A. Group Ltd., Melbourne	–
Chase-N.B.A. New Zealand Group Ltd., New Zealand	–
Flagship Pacific Holdings, Wellington	–

J.P. Morgan & Co. Inc.

Australian United Corporation Ltd., Melbourne	21%
Financial Leasing Corporation (Australia) Ltd., Melbourne	35%
First New Zealand International Ltd., Wellington	5%

Chemical New York Corporation

Development Underwriting Ltd., Sydney	10%

Name	Percentage held
Bankers Trust New York Corporation	
Ord-Bank & Trust Company, Sydney	90%
Continental Illinois Corporation	
Commercial Continental Ltd., Sydney	–
First National Boston Corporation	
Boston Financial Ltd., Melbourne	100%
First Leasing Australia Ltd., Melbourne	50%
Marine Midland Banks Inc.	
Midland Credit Ltd., Sydney	15%
Patrick-Intermarine (Australia) Ltd., Australia	20%
Bremner Intermarine (N.Z.) Ltd., New Zealand	20%
Mellon National Corporation	
Network Finance Ltd., Sydney	20%
Security Pacific National Bank	
Marac Holdings Ltd., Auckland	20%
Tricontinental Corporation Ltd., Melbourne	24%
Wells Fargo & Co.	
Broadbank Corporation, New Zealand	12%
Martin Corporation Group Ltd., Sydney	40%
Western Bancorporation	
Euro-Pacific Finance Corporation Ltd.	12.5%

Notes
1. Held by Bank of America N.T. & S.A.
2. Held by Bamerical International Financial Corp.

Sources
Banks' annual reports for 1974; and The Banker Research Unit: *Who owns what in world banking 1974-75,* London, September 1974.

APPENDIX 3

The British clearing banks' international links

Name	Capital	Percentage held

Barclays Bank Ltd.[1]

Banca Barclays Castellini S.p.A. (Italy)	500.000 Mill. Lit	75.0 %
Banco del Desarrollo Económico Español (Spain)		6.0 %
Banque de Bruxelles S.A., Brussels		3.0 %
Banque de la Société Financière Européenne, "BSFE", Paris	50.00 Mill. FF	12.5%
Barclays Bank S.A., Paris (with branches in France and Monaco)	37.00 Mill. FF	100.0 %
Barclays Finance Corporation (Cyprus) Ltd., Cyprus	0.050 Mill. Z £	100.0 %
Barclays Finance Corporation (Malta) Ltd., Malta	0.150 Mill. M £	100.0 %
Barclays Kol & Co. N.V., (Netherlands)	7.668 Mill. florins	79.53%
Hellenic Mutual Fund Management Co. S.A. (Greece)	5.00 Mill. Drs	24.0 %
Intercredit S.A. (Belgium)	20 Mill. bfrs	100.0 %
International Nuclear Credit Corporation (Luxembourg)		11.0 %
Investment Bank of Malta Ltd., Malta	0.125 Mill. M £	60.0 %
Mercur Bank S.A., Luxembourg		16.6 %
Nordbank AG, Hamburg		25.0 %
Société Bancaire Barclays (Suisse) S.A., Geneva	20.000 Mill. sfrs	51.0 %
Société Financière Européenne, "S.F.E.", Luxembourg	160.000 Mill. bfrs	12.5 %
Société Immobilière Fleurs Belles 'A' (Switzerland)		100.0 %
Vermögens-, Verwertungs- und Verwaltungs-GmbH (Germany)		100.0 %

Name	*Capital*	*Percentage held*

Midland Bank Ltd.

Banque Européenne de Crédit, "B.E.C.", Brussels	1,332.000 Mill. bfrs	13.12%
Thos. Cook & Son Société Anonyme (Belgium)		59.0 %
Europäisch-Asiatische Bank AG (Germany)		17.0 %
European Banks' International Company S.A., "E.B.I.C.", Brussels	175.000 Mill. bfrs	14.3 %
European Enterprises Development Co. S.A., "E.E.D." Luxembourg	15.40 Mill. US $	ca. 1.0%
Malta International Banking Corporation Ltd., Malta		13.0 %
Northern Bank Finance Corporation Ltd., Dublin	0.10 Mill. £	100.0 %[2]
Northern Bank Trustee Company Ltd., Dublin		100.0 %
SIFIDA Société Internationale Financière pour les Investissements et le Développement en Afrique, Luxembourg	50.000 Mill. US $	ca. 2 %

National Westminster Bank Ltd.

Banca Milanese di Credito, Milan	1,750.000 Mill. Lit	31.0 %
Handelsbank, Zurich		55.0 %
Van Lanschot's Beleggings Co. B.V., Eindhoven	55.000 Mill. hfl	25.0 %
Orion Leasing Holdings Ltd., London	1.98 Mill. £	16.67%
Multinational Orion Leasing Holdings N.V., Amsterdam	78.000 Mill. hfl	16.67%
Libra Bank Ltd., London	6.3 Mill. £	5.0 %
Orion Bank Ltd., London	22.5 Mill. £	20.0 %

133

Name	Capital	Percentage held
Union Financière et Bancaire S.A., Paris	200.000 Mill. FF	20.0 %

Lloyds Bank Ltd.³

Name	Capital	Percentage held
Bax' Bank N.V., Netherlands		100.0 %
Etablissement Dormit (Liechtenstein)		100.0 %
Etablissement Pro Fide (Liechtenstein)		100.0 %
Gillissen Jonker & Co. N.V. (Netherlands)		100.0 %
Lloyds & Bolsa International Management S.A. (Switzerland)		60.0 %
Lloyds Bank (Belgium) S.A. (Belgium)		100.0 %
Lloyds Bank (Cannes) S.A. (France)		99.0 %

Name	Capital	Percentage held
Barclays Bank Ltd.		
Barclays Bank of California, San Francisco	10.000 Mill. US $	100.0 %
Barclays Bank of New York, New York	2.600 Mill. US $	99.82%
Barclays (Canada) Ltd. (Canada)	5.050 Mill. C $	100.0 %
Bermuda Provident Bank Ltd., Bermuda	0.720 Mill. BD $	31.12 %
Export Leasing Company (Bermuda)		33.33%
International Trust Company of Bermuda Ltd., Bermuda	0.220 Mill. BD $	20.0 %
Midland Bank Ltd.		
Bank of Bermuda		9.1 %
Thos. Cook & Son Incorporates (USA)		59.0 %
European-American Bank & Trust Company, New York	60.0 Mill. US $	18.38%
European-American Banking Corporation, New York	19.000 Mill. US $	20.13%

Name	Capital	Percentage held
Barclays Bank Ltd.		
Bahamas International Trust Co. Ltd. (Bahamas)	1.000 Mill. Bahama $	26.0%
Banco Popular Antiliano N.V. (Netherlands Antilles)	1.708 Mill. N.A. fls	53.3 %
Barcair Ltd. (Barbados)	–	100.0 %
Barclays Bank of Jamaica Ltd., Jamaica	–	100.0 %
Barclays Bank of Trinidad and Tobago Ltd. (Trinidad and Tobago)	2.700 Mill. TT $	100.0 %
Barclays Finance Corporation (Bahamas) Ltd. (Bahamas)	0.150 Mill. Bahama $	100.0 %
Barclays Finance Corporation of Barbados Ltd. (Barbados)	0.250 Mill. EC $	100.0 %
Barclays Finance Corporation of Jamaica Ltd. (Jamaica)	0.400 Mill. J $	100.0 %
Barclays Finance Corporation of Trinidad and Tobago Ltd. (Trinidad and Tobago)	1.250 Mill. TT $	100.0 %
Barclays Finance Corporation of the Cayman Islands	–	100.0 %
Cayman International Trust Co. Ltd. (Cayman Islands)	0.400 Mill. C.I. $	26.0 %
Eagle Services Ltd., Grand Cayman	–	100.0 %
Financiadora B.C.N., S.A., Brazil	–	33.3 %
National Westminster Bank Ltd.		
Roy West Banking Corporation Ltd., Nassau (Bahamas)	17.160 Mill. Bahama $	40.0 %

Name	Capital	Percentage held

Lloyds Bank Ltd.

Name	Capital	Percentage held
Banco Novo Rio de Investi-mentos S.A. (Brazil)		50.0 %
Bank of London & Mont-real Ltd. (Bahamas)		100.0 %
B.O.L.S.A. Empreendimentos Comerciais Ltda. (Brazil)		100.0 %
Bolsa Ltd. (Bahamas)		100.0 %
S.A. Comercial Anglo-Ecuato-riana (Ecuador)		100.0 %
Compañia Administradora de Londres y Rio de la Plata y El Cabildo Cia. Argentina de Seguros S.A. (Argentina)		100.0 %
Compañia Financiera de Lon-dres S.A. (Argentina)		95.0 %
Compañia Investiones Aban-cay (Peru)		9.0 %
Compañia Inversiones 'La Escocesa' Ltda. (Chile)		100.0 %
Corporación Financiera Colom-biana (Colombia)		8.0 %
Corporación Financiera Nacional (Colombia)		8.0 %
Gerlonsa S.A. Gerente de Fondosa Comunes de Inversión (Argentina)		100.0 %
Importada Industrial 'Bulnes' S.A.C. (Chile)		99.0 %
Intercontinental Data Services, S.A.C.I. (Argentina)		100.0 %
Laida S.A. Comercial Immobilia-ria y Financiera (Argentina)		100.0 %
LBI Bank & Trust Co. (Cayman) Ltd. (Cayman Islands)		100.0 %
Londres y Rio de la Plata Cia. Argentina de Seguros S.A. (Argentina)		75.0 %

Name	Capital	Percentage held
Milne & Co. S.A. (Peru)		100.0 %
Monteprop S.A. (Uruguay)		100.0 %
Servinco S.A. – Servicos de Informacoes Cadastrais e Cobrancas (Brazil)		100.0 %

Name	Capital	Percentage held
Barclays Bank Ltd.		
Banque Internationale pour le Commerce et l'Industrie du Cameroun S.A., Yaounde	750.000 Mill. CFA-Francs	27.62%
Banque Malgache d'Escompte et de Crédit S.A. (Bames) (Madagascar)	750.000 Mill. FMg	12.0 %
Barclays Bank of Ghana Ltd. (Ghana)	4.000 Mill. shares	100.0 %
Barclays Bank International Executor & Trust Co. (Private) Ltd. (Rhodesia)		100.0 %
Barclays Bank of Nigeria Ltd., Lagos (with 82 branches in Nigeria)	12.000 Mill. N £	52.0 %
Barclays Bank of Sierra Leone Ltd. (Sierra Leone)	0.640 Mill. Le	87.50%
Barclays Bank of Swaziland Ltd.	–	60.0 %
Barclays Bank of Uganda Ltd., Kampala (with 42 branches in Uganda)	20.000 Mill. U Shs	51.0 %
Barclays Bank of Zambia Ltd. (Zambia)	3.000 Mill. SK	100.0 %
Barclays Bank S.Z.A.R.L. (Zaire)	0.040 Mill. shares	100.0 %
Barclays Discount Bank Ltd. (Israel)	11.000 Mill. I £	50.10%
Barclays Insurance Brokers South Africa Ltd. (South-Africa)	0.010 Mill. Rs	100.0 %
Barclays National Bank Ltd. (South-Africa)	40.000 Mill. Rs	100.0 %
Barclays National Investments (Proprietary) Ltd. (South-Africa)	0.100 Mill. Rs	100.0 %
Barclays South African Investments Ltd.		

Name	Capital	Percentage held
(South-Africa)	0.415 Mill. Rs	100.0 %
East African Acceptances Ltd. (Kenya)	5.000 Mill. K.Shs	30.0 %
National Bank Development and Investment Corporation Ltd. (South-Africa)	2.500 Mill. Rs	100.0 %
National Bank of Malawi (Malawi)	1.000 Mill. MK	25.0 %
National Bank of South Africa Ltd.	–	100.0 %

Midland Bank Ltd.

Thos. Cook & Son (South Africa) Pty. Ltd. (South Africa)	–	59.0 %

Lloyds Bank Ltd.

Mauritius Commercial Bank Finance Corporation Ltd. (Mauritius)	5.000 Mill. Rs	40.0 %
The Mauritius Commercial Bank Ltd.	6.000 Mill. Rs	16.6 %

Name	Capital	Percentage held
Barclays Bank Ltd.		
Asiadata Ltd., Hong Kong		9.0 %
Trident International Finance Ltd., Hong Kong	20.000 Mill. HK $	33.33%
Midland Bank Ltd.		
Private Investment Company for Asia (Pica) S.A., Tokyo/Panama-City	25.4 Mill. US $	1.0 %
National Westminster Bank Ltd.		
Orion Pacific Ltd., Hong Kong	62.500 Mill. HK $	15.0 %

141

Name	Capital	Percentage held
Barclays Bank Ltd.		
Barclays Australia Holdings Ltd. (Australia)	0.435 Mill. A $	100.0 %
Barclays Australia Ltd. (Australia)	5.000 Mill. A $	100.0 %
Barclays International Australia Ltd. (Australia)		100.0 %
Barclays International New Zealand Ltd. (New Zealand)		100.0 %
Barrep Pty. Ltd. (Australia)		100.0 %
Melanesia International Trust Co. Ltd. (New Hebrides)	15.000 Mill. p	17.67%
New Zealand United Corporation Ltd., Wellington	1.560 Mill. NZ $	20.0 %
Midland Bank Ltd.		
Euro-Pacific Finance Corporation Ltd., Melbourne	2.5 Mill. A $	15.5 %
Thos. Cook & Son Pty. Ltd. (Australia)		59.0 %
National Westminster Bank Ltd.		
Lombard Australia Ltd. (Australia)		100.0 %
Lombard New Zealand Ltd. (New Zealand)		100.0 %
Lloyds Bank Ltd.		
Burns Philip & International Trustee Co. Ltd. (New Hebrides)		6.0 %
Databank System Ltd. (New Zealand)	0.200 Mill. NZ $	20.0 %[2]

142

Name	Capital	Percentage held
General Finance Ltd. (New Zealand)	2.988 Mill. NZ $	21.5 %[2]
Lloyds & Bolsa Australia Ltd. (Australia)		100.0 %
National Bank of New Zealand Savings Bank Ltd. (New Zealand)		
South Pacific Merchant Finance Ltd. (New Zealand)		52.5 %

Notes
1. Including foreign subsidiaries and participations of Barclays Bank International, a wholly-owned subsidiary of Barclays Bank Ltd.
2. Indirect.
3. Including foreign subsidiaries and participations of Lloyds Bank International Ltd.

Sources
Banks' annual reports for 1974; The Banker Research unit: *Who owns what in world banking 1974-75,* London, September 1974; and the files of the HWWA Institut für Wirtschaftsforschung-Hamburg.

APPENDIX 4

German banks abroad

a) Subsidiaries and principal interests of German banks in foreign financial institutions
b) Foreign branches of German banks
c) Representative offices of German banks abroad

a) SUBSIDIARIES AND PRINCIPAL INTERESTS OF GERMAN BANKS IN FOREIGN FINANCIAL INSTITUTIONS

EUROPE		*End 1974*
Name	*Capital*	*Percentage held*

Commerzbank

Name	Capital		Percentage held
ADELA Investment Company S.A., Luxembourg/Lima	61.28	Mill. US $	1.4 %
Atlas Participations – France S.A.R.L., Paris	10.50	Mill. FF	100.0 %
Banco Urquijo S.A., Madrid	4,860.67	Mill. Ptas	0.8 %
Bontrade, Brussels/New York	5.00	Mill. US $	8.8 %
Commerzbank International S.A., Luxembourg	790.000	Mill. lfrs	100.0 %
Crédit Chimique S.A., Paris	34.00	Mill. FF	10.0 %
Europartners Bank (Nederland) N.V., Amsterdam	40.00	Mill. hfl	60.0 %
Europartenaires Leasing S.A., Paris	0.10	Mill FF	33.3 %
European Enterprises Development Company S.A., (E.E.D.), Luxembourg	15.40	Mill. US $	1.4 %
Finanzierungsgesellschaft VIKING, Zurich	45.00	Mill sfrs	6.7 %
Finatourinvest S.A., Luxembourg	194.60	Mill. lfrs	0.6 %
Gestinver S.A., Madrid	187.50	Mill. Ptas	2.5 %
International Commercial Bank Ltd., (I.C.B.), London	5.00	Mill. £	12.0 %
International Investment Corporation for Yugoslavia S.A., Luxembourg	13.50	Mill. US $	1.2 %
IRIS-Institutional Research and Investment Services, S.A., Geneva	0.90	Mill. sfrs	33.3 %
SIFIDA Société Internationale Financière pour les Investissements et le Dé-			

Name	Capital		Percentage held
veloppement en Afrique S.A., Luxembourg	12.50	Mill. US $	0.8 %
Société de Gestion du Rominvest International Fund S.A., Luxembourg	35.00	Mill. lfrs	10.0 %
Société Européenne d'Edition et de Diffusion S.A., Luxembourg	0.82	Mill. FF	6.1 %
Teollistamisrahasto Oy— Industrialization Fund of Finland Ltd., Helsinki	40.00	Mill. Fmk	0.6 %
U.B.A.E. Union de Banques Arabes et Européennes S.A., Luxembourg/Frankfurt	30.00	Mill. DM	13.7 %
Wobaco Holding Company, Luxembourg	21.60	Mill. US $	2.7 %

Deutsche Bank

Name	Capital		Percentage held
ADELA Investment Company S.A., Luxembourg/Lima	61.28	Mill. US $	0.7 %
Banco Comercial Transatlántico, Barcelona	801.0	Mill. Ptas	25.5 %
Banco del Desarrollo Económico Español S.A., Madrid	899.8	Mill. Ptas	1.9 %
Banco Español en Alemania S.A., Madrid	165.0	Mill. Ptas	15.0 %
Banque Européenne de Crédit, BEC, Brussels	1,425.3	Mill. bfrs	14.3 %
H. Albert de Bary & Co. N.V., Amsterdam	15.0	Mill. hfl	20.0 %
Compagnie Financière de la Deutsche Bank AG, Luxembourg	900.0	Mill. lfrs	99.9 %
EDESA S.A. Holding, Luxembourg	11.0	Mill. US $	4.6 %
European Arab Bank (Brussels) S.A., Brussels European-Arab Holding S.A., Luxembourg	1,000.0	Mill. lfrs	5.7 %

147

Name	*Capital*	*Percentage held*
European Banking Company Ltd., London	10.0 Mill. £	14.3 %
European Banks' International Company S.A., EBIC, Brussels	175.0 Mill. bfrs	14.3 %
European Brazilian Bank Ltd., (EUROBRAZ), London	4.2 Mill. £	10.4 %
European Financial Associates N.V., The Hague	0.4 Mill. hfl	14.3 %
European Hotel Corporation (EHC) N.V., Amsterdam	41.2 Mill. hfl	5.4 %
International Investment Corporation for Yugoslavia S.A., Luxembourg	13.5 Mill. US $	1.2 %
International Mexican Bank Ltd., London	5.0 Mill. £	7.2 %
Iran Overseas Investment Bank Ltd., London	5.0 Mill. £	10.0 %
Nationale Investitionsbank für Industrieentwicklung AG, Athens	450.0 Mill. Drs	5.3 %
Promotora de Edificios para Oficinas S.A., Barcelona	180.0 Mill. Ptas	25.2 %
Société Internationale Financière pour les Investissements et le Développement en Afrique S.A. (SIFIDA), Luxembourg	12.5 Mill. US $	0.8 %
Teollistamisrahasto Oy — Industrialization Fund of Finland Ltd., Helsinki	48.0 Mill. Fmk	0.7 %

Deutsche Ueberseeische Bank[1]

ADELA Investment Company S.A., Luxembourg/Lima	61.28 Mill. US $	0.07%
Compagnie Financière de la Deutsche Bank AG,		

148

Name	Capital	Percentage held
Luxembourg	900.0 Mill. lfrs	0.0024%

Dresdner Bank

Name	Capital	Percentage held
ADELA Investment Company S.A., Luxembourg/Lima	61.28 Mill. US $	0.8 %
Associated Banks' of Europe Corporation S.A., (ABECOR), Brussels	7.0 Mill. bfrs	14.3 %
Banco de Financiación Industrial S.A., (INDUBAN), Madrid	1,301.75 Mill. Ptas	3.0 %
Banque de la Société Financière Européenne, (B.S.F.E.), Paris	200.0 Mill. FF	1.5 %
Compagnie Luxembourgeoise de Banque S.A., (CLB), Luxembourg	1,500.0 Mill. lfrs	99.9 %
EDESA S.A., Luxembourg	11.0 Mill. US $	4.6 %
EUROFINANCE S.A., Paris	2.203 Mill. FF	12.3 %
Euro-Latinamerican Bank Ltd., (EULA BANK), London	12.0 Mill. £	5.0 %
European Enterprises Development Company, E.E.D., S.A., Luxembourg/Paris	19.409 Mill. US $	2.1 %
European International Fund Management Company S.A., Luxembourg	8.0 Mill. lfrs	24.9 %
Financiera Hispaña Internacional S.A., (FINTER), Madrid	350.0 Mill. Ptas	10.0 %
Finanztrust AG, Glarus	0.25 Mill. sfrs	100.0 %
International Energy Bank Ltd., (I.E.B.), London[2]		
The International Investment Corporation for Yugoslavia S.A., Luxembourg, Zagreb	13.50 Mill. US $	1.2 %
International Nuclear Finance Holding, I.N.F.H.,		

Name	Capital		Percentage held
Luxembourg Investment Bank S.A.,	10.0	Mill. US $	10.0 %
Athens	300.0	Mill. Drs	1.0 %
Société Financière Euro-péenne — S.F.E. —, Luxembourg	160.0	Mill. bfrs	12.5 %
Société Financière pour les Pays d'Outre-Mer S.A., (S.F.O.M.), Geneva, Paris	55.0	Mill. sfrs	15.0 %
Teollistamisrahasto Oy — Industrialization Fund of Finland Ltd., Helsinki	48.0	Mill. Fmk	1.1 %
Touristik Finanz AG, Baden/Switzerland	20.0	Mill. sfrs	20.0 %

Deutsch-Südamerikanische Bank[3]

ADELA Investment Company S.A., Luxembourg/Lima	61.28	Mill. US $	0.2 %
Euro-Latinamerican Bank Ltd. (EULA-BANK), London	12.0	Mill. £	2.0 %

Westdeutsche Landesbank — Girozentrale

ADELA Investment Company S.A., Luxembourg/Lima	61.28	Mill. US $	0.89%
Bank der Bondsspaarbanken N.V., Amsterdam	25.0	Mill. hfl	5.0 %
Banque Franco-Allemande S.A., Paris, (indirect)	30.0	Mill. FF	over 25%
Banque de l'Union Euro-péenne, Paris, (indirect)	0.154	Mill. FF	4.7 %
Banque Nordeurope S.A., Luxembourg, (through West LB International, Luxembourg)	300.0	Mill. lfrs	50.0 %
Interspar-Verwaltungsgesell-schaft S.A., Luxembourg	5.0	Mill. lfrs	26.6 %
International Investment Corporation for Yugoslavia S.A. (IICY), Luxembourg	13.5	Mill. US $	1.56%

Name	Capital		Percentage held
Kredietbank S.A. Luxembourgeoise, Luxembourg	300.0	Mill. bfrs	6.0 %
Libra Bank Ltd., London	6.3	Mill. £	10.61%
Orion Bank Ltd., London	22.5	Mill. £	20.0 %
Orion Leasing Holdings Ltd., London	1.98	Mill. £	16.67%
Orion Multinational Services Ltd., London	0.450	Mill. £	16.67%
Multinational Orion Leasing Holdings N.V., Amsterdam	78.0	Mill. hfl	16.67%
Société Internationale Financière pour les Investissements et le Développement en Afrique S.A. (SIFIDA), Luxembourg	12.5	Mill. US $	0.8 %
U.B.A.E. Union de Banques Arabes et Européennes S.A., Luxembourg	30.0	Mill. DM	9.8 %
WestLB International S.A., Luxembourg	1,500.0	Mill. lfrs	100.0 %

Bayerische Hypotheken- und Wechsel-Bank

Associated Banks' of Europe Corporation S.A., (ABECOR), Brussels	7.0	Mill. bfrs	14.3 %
Banco Atlántico S.A., Barcelona[4]	2,461.694	Mill. Ptas	5.0 %
Bank für Kärnten AG, Klagenfurt	100.0	Mill. öS	10.0 %
Euro-Latinamerican Bank Ltd. (EULA-BANK), London	12.0	Mill. £	5.0 %
Hypo-Bank International S.A., Luxembourg	600.0	Mill. lfrs	99.9 %
United International Bank Ltd., London	6.0	Mill. £	10.0 %

Bayerische Vereinsbank

Banco Europeo de Negocios,   less than

151

Name	Capital		Percentage held
Eurobanco, Madrid	1,276	Mill. Ptas	25%
Bank für Oberösterreich und Salzburg, Linz	125	Mill. öS	less than 25%
Bank für Tirol und Voralberg AG, Innsbruck	100	Mill. öS	less than 25%
Banque de l'Union Européenne, Paris	154.292	Mill. FF	less than 25%
Bayerische Vereinsbank International S.A., Luxembourg	500.0	Mill. lfrs	ca. 100%
Crédit du Nord et de l'Union Parisienne "C.N.U.P.", Paris	240.0	Mill. FF	5.0 %
EFIBANCA – Ente Finanziario Interbancario S.p.A., Rome	20,000	Mill. L	less than 25%
GATX International Finance Inc., Zug	45.0	Mill. sfrs	less than 25%
Noreco Finanz AG, Zürich	20.0	Mill. sfrs	7.0 %
SIFIDA Société Internationale Financière pour les Investissements et le Développement en Afrique, Luxembourg	12.5	Mill. US $	less than 25%
Société Européenne d'Etudes pour le Financement d'Airbus S.A.R.L., Paris	–		less than 25%
U.B.A.E. Union de Banques Arabes et Européennes S.A., Luxembourg	30.0	Mill. DM	less than 25%
Union Internationale de Financement et de Participation, "INTERUNION", Paris	38.0	Mill. FF	7.0 %

Vereins- und Westbank

Aktiengesellschaft für Kapitalanlagen und kommerzielle Finanzierungen, Vaduz	1.35	Mill. sfrs	over 25%

Name	*Capital*		*Percentage held*
Noreco Finanz AG, Zürich	20.0	Mill. sfrs	7.0 %
Vereins- und Westbank Internationale Société Anonyme, Luxembourg	350.0	Mill. lfrs	100.0 %

BHF-Bank

BHF-BANK – DGK International S.A., Luxembourg	600.0	Mill. lfrs	60.0 %
Brown Harriman & International Banks Limited, London	3.88	Mill. £	6.02%
Compagnie Bruxelles Lambert pour le Finance et l'Industrie S.A., Brussels	3,924.5	Mill. bfrs	less than 1%
Crédit Commercial de France, Paris	258.4	Mill. FF	1.5 %
Euro-Clearance Systems Ltd., London	2.5	Mill. US $	1.25%
Eurosyndicat S.A., Luxembourg	10.0	Mill. lfrs	10.0 %
"Mediobanca" Banca di Credito Finanziario S.p.A., Milan	222,400.0	Mill. Lit	less than 1 %
BHF-Bank FINANCE (Holding), Luxembourg	2.50	Mill. DM	100.0 %
BHF-FINANZ-Gesellschaft, Zurich	1.0	Mill. sfrs	100.0 %
INTER-ALPHA ASIA, Luxembourg	10.0	Mill. US $	14.29%

M.M. Warburg-Brinckmann, Wirtz & Co.

S.G. Warburg & Co. International Holdings Ltd., London	–		–
M.M. Warburg-Brinckmann, Wirtz International S.A., Luxembourg	200.0	Mill. lfrs	100.0 %

Name	Capital		Percentage held
Commerzbank			
Europartners Securities Corporation, New York	3.27	Mill. US $	30.6 %
Deutsche Bank			
European-American Banking Corporation, New York, Los Angeles, San Francisco	19.0	Mill. US $	20.125%
European-American Banking & Trust Company, New York	60.0	Mill. US $	18.375%
German American Capital Corporation, Baltimore	0.01	Mill. US $	100.0 %
UBS-DB Corporation, New York	0.1	Mill. US $	50.0 %
Dresdner Bank			
A.B.D. Securities Corporation, Dover, Delaware, New York	5.0	Mill. US $	25.0 %
Bayerische Hypotheken- und Wechsel-Bank			
A.B.D. Securities Corporation, New York/Boston	5.0	Mill. US $	25.0 %
Vereins- und Westbank			
The Metropolitan Trust Company, Toronto	10.0	Mill. can. $	under 25%

Name	Capital		Percentage held

Commerzbank

Name	Capital		Percentage held
Banco de Investimento do Brasil S.A. (B.I.B.), Rio de Janeiro	120.96	Mill. Cr $	5.0 %
Deltec Panamerica S.A., Nassau (Bahamas)	5.13	Mill. shares	1.9 %

Deutsche Bank

Name	Capital		Percentage held
Banco Bradesco de Investimento S.A., São Paulo	341.9	Mill. Cr $	5.0 %
Corporación Financiera Colombiana, S.A., (COFINANCIERA), Bogotá	156.9	Mill. col. $	0.4 %

Deutsche Ueberseeische Bank

Name	Capital		Percentage held
Banco Itaú de Investimentos S.A., São Paulo	129	Mill. Cr $	1.897%
Banco de Montevideo, Montevideo	350	Mill. urug $	43.34 %
Companhia Brasileira de Entrepostos e Comercio, "COBEC", São Paulo	120	Mill. Cr $	0.83 %
Compañia de Mandatos Inmobiliaria y Financiera S.A., Buenos Aircs	1.0	Mill. argent $	100.0 %
IMOBAL – Imobiliária e Administradora Ltda., São Paulo	1.53	Mill. Cr $	100.0 %
Compañia Paraguaya de Desarrollo S.A., "COMDESA", Asunción	161.960	Mill. G.	2.333%

Dresdner Bank

Name	Capital		Percentage held
Corporación Financiera Colombiana S.A., (COFINCIERA), Bogotá	156.87	Mill. col. $	0.4 %

155

Name	Capital	Percentage held

Deutsch-Südamerikanische Bank

Name	Capital	Percentage held
Atlantic Bank Limited, Belize	0.500 Mill. BZ $	13.3 %
Banco Argentino de Comercio, Buenos Aires	19.7 Mill. argent. $	21.99 %
Banco del Comercio, Bogotá/Panamá	280 Mill. col. $	5 %
Banco FINASA de Investimento S.A., São Paulo	135 Mill. Cr $	1.79 %
Banco Lar Brasileiro S.A., Rio de Janeiro/São Paulo	99 Mill. Cr $	10 %
Banco de Investimentos Lar Brasileiro S.A., Rio de Janeiro	35.445 Mill. Cr $	5 %
Compañia General de Inversiones S.A.F., Buenos Aires	1.879 Mill. argent. $	6.666%
Compañia Paraguaya de Desarrollo S.A., "COMDESA", Asunción	161.960 Mill. G.	2.5 %
Corporación Nicaraguense de Inversiones, Managua		
COTINCO, Companhia de Organizacão Técnica, Industrial e Commercial, São Paulo/Rio de Janeiro	0.380 Mill. Cr $	100.0 %
COTINCO, Consultora Técnica, Industrial y Comercial S.A., México	0.600 Mill. mex. pes.	100.0 %
Crédito Argentino Germánico S.A. Financiera, Commercial e Industrial, Buenos Aires	0.150 Mill. argent. $	100.0 %
Crédito Germánico S.A., Montevideo	0.100 Mill. DM	100.0 %
Financiera Industrial y Agropecuaria S.A., "FIASA", Ciudad de Guatemala	2 Mill. Q.	2.5 %

Name	*Capital*		*Percentage held*
C.A. Venezolana de Desarrollo (Sociedad Financiera), Caracas	40	Mill. B.	0.7545%
Bayerische Vereinsbank			
Deltec Panamerica S.A., Nassau (Bahamas)	5.13	Mill. shares	less than 25%
INTERUNION Antilles N.V., Curaçao	15.0	Mill. $	less than 25%
Banco Itaú de Investimentos S.A., São Paulo	129.0	Mill. Cr $	less than 25%

Name	Capital		Percentage held

Commerzbank

Banque Marocaine du Com- merce Extérieur, Casa- blanca	40.00	Mill. DH	2.8 %
Banque Nationale pour le Développement Economique, Rabat	32.40	Mill. DH	0.7 %
The Commercial Bank of Dubai Ltd., Dubaı	11.00	Mill. QDR	20.0 %
Nigerian Industrial De- velopment Bank Ltd., Lagos	4.50	Mill. N-£	1.7 %
Rifbank S.A.L., Beirut	4.00	Mill. L-£	31.8 %
Société Financière de Dé- veloppement – SOFIDE – Kinshasa (Zaire)	2.00	Mill. Zaires	2.5 %
Société Libano Européenne pour la Gestion Privée (Crédit Lyonnais) S.A.L., SLIGEST, Beirut	2.00	Mill. L-£	5.0 %
Union Internationale de Banques S.A., Tunis	2.00	Mill. tD	4.0 %

Deutsche Bank

Banque Commerciale Congo- laise, Brazzaville	700.0	Mill. FCFA	3.1 %
Banque Commerciale du Maroc, Casablanca	19.5	Mill. DH	7.2 %
Banque Nationale pour le Développement Economique, Rabat	32.4	Mill. DH	0.7 %
Banque Tchadienne de Cré- dit et de Dépôts, N'Djamena/Tchad	330.0	Mill. FCFA	7.5 %
Société Camerounaise de Banque, Yaoundé	1,500.0	Mill. FCFA	5.0 %
Société Ivoirienne de Banque, Abidjan	1,000.0	Mill. FCFA	12.0 %

Name	Capital		Percentage held
Union Gabonaise de Banque, Libreville	750.0	Mill. FCFA	10.0 %
Union Sénégalaise de Banque pour le Commerce et l'Industrie, Dakar	1,000.0	Mill. FCFA	3.8 %
Union Togolaise de Banque, Lome/Togo	400.0	Mill. FCFA	18.0 %

Dresdner Bank

Banque Nationale pour le Développement Economique, Rabat	32.4	Mill. DH	0.7 %

Bayerische Vereinsbank

Banque de Paris et de Pays-Bas (Zaire), Kinshasa (Zaire)	0.726	Mill. Zaires	25.0 %
Banque de Tunisie S.A., Tunis	1.5	Mill. tun Di.	less than 25%
Société Générale de Banques au Cameroun S.A., Yaoundé	1,125	Mill. FCFA	less than 25%
Société Internationale de Particip. et de Gestion (holding company for "l'Union Congolaise de Banques"), Brazzaville	200.0	Mill. FCFA	less than 25%
Société Générale de Banques au Sénégal S.A., Dakar	825	Mill. FCFA	less than 25%
Société Générale de Banques en Côte d'Ivoire S.A., Abidjan	1,500	Mill. FCFA	less than 25%
Société Mauritanienne de Banques S.A., Nouakchott	50.0	Mill. oug.	less than 25%

BHF-Bank

Bidi Banque Ivoirienne de

Name	Capital		Percentage held
Développement Industriel, Abidjan	1,050.0	Mill. FCFA	1.79%
National Investment Bank, Accra (Ghana)	18.0	Mill. NC	less than 1 %

Name	Capital		Percentage held

Commerzbank

Name	Capital		Percentage held
The Development Bank of Singapore Ltd., Singapore	100.00	Mill. S $	0.5%
P.T. Finconesia, Financial Corporation of Indonesia, Jakarta	600.00	Mill. Rp	10.0%
The Industrial Finance Corporation of Thailand (IFCT), Bangkok	150.00	Mill. Baht	2.0%
Mithai Europartners Finance and Investment Ltd., Bangkok	10.00	Mill. Baht	10.0%
Nippon Europartners Consulting Company, Tokyo	100.00	Mill. yen	25.0%
The Pakistan Industrial Credit and Investment Corporation Limited, Karachi	70.00	Mill. pRs	0.4 %
Private Investment Company for Asia (PICA) S.A., Tokyo, Panama	28.20	Mill. US $	0.7 %

Deutsche Bank

Name	Capital		Percentage held
AEA Development Corporation, Manila/Philippines	30.0	Mill. phil. Pes.	6.0%
Foreign Trade Bank of Iran, Teheran	700.0	Mill. Rials	11.8%
Industrial and Mining Development Bank of Iran, Teheran	3,150.0	Mill. Rials	0.9%
The Industrial Credit and Investment Corporation of India Ltd., Bombay	150.0	Mill. iRs	1.5%
The Industrial Finance Corporation of Thailand, Bangkok	150.0	Mill. Baht	2.9%

Name	Capital		Percentage held
Korea Development Finance Corporation, Seoul	3,000.0	Mill. Won	2.5%
Malaysian Industrial Development Finance Berhad, Kuala Lumpur	74.1	Mill. M-$	0.5%
The Pakistan Industrial Credit and Investment CorporationLtd., Karachi	66.4	Mill. pRs	4.8%
Private Development Corporation of the Philippines, Makati, Rizal	40.25	Mill. phil. Pes.	1.8%
Private Investment Company for Asia (PICA) S.A., Tokyo, Panama	28.2	Mill. US $	0.7%

Dresdner Bank

Name	Capital		Percentage held
Asian and Euro-American Capital Corporation (Thailand) Ltd., Bangkok	40.0	Mill. Baht	10.0%
P.T. Asian and Euro-American Capital Corporation Ltd., Jakarta	300.0	Mill. Rp	8.3%
Asian and Euro-American Merchant Bank Ltd., Singapore	24.41	Mill. S $	11.0%
Asian and Euro-American Merchant Bankers (Malaysia) Berhad, Kuala Lumpur	7.0	Mill. M-$	5.5%
Development and Investment Bank of Iran (DIBI), Teheran	2,100.0	Mill. Rials	4.8%
The Development Bank of Singapore Ltd., Singapore	100.0	Mill. S $	0.5%
Dresdner (South East Asia) Ltd., Singapore	7.0	Mill. S $	100.0%
The Industrial Credit and Investment Corpo-			

Name	Capital		Percentage held
ration of India Ltd., (ICICI), Bombay	150.0	Mill. iRs	1.3%
The Pakistan Industrial Credit and Investment Corporation Ltd., (PICIC), Karachi	70.0	Mill. pRs	0.1%
Private Investment Company for Asia (PICA) S.A., Tokyo, Panama	28.2	Mill. US $	0.7%

Westdeutsche Landesbank-Girozentrale

Orion Pacific Ltd., Hongkong	62.5	Mill. HK-$	15 %

Bayerische Vereinsbank

The Pakistan Industrial Credit and Investment Corporation Ltd., (PICIC), Karachi	70.0	Mill. pRs	less than 25%

Vereins- und Westbank

The Development Bank of Singapore Ltd., Singapore	200.0	Mill. S $	less than 25%

BHF-Bank

The Pakistan Industrial Credit and Investment Corporation Ltd., Karachi	70.0	Mill. pRs	less than 1%

M.M. Warburg-Brinckmann, Wirtz & Co.

The Development Bank of Singapore Ltd., Singapore	100.0	Mill. S $	–

Name	Capital	Percentage held
Commerzbank		
Australian United Corporation Ltd., Melbourne	5.11 Mill. A $	6.4%
Deutsche Bank		
Euro-Pacific Finance Corporation Ltd., Melbourne	5.0 Mill. A $	8.0%
Dresdner Bank		
Australian European Finance Corporation Ltd., (A.E.F.C.), Sydney	10.0 Mill. A $	18.0%
M.M. Warburg-Brinckmann, Wirtz & Co.		
Australian United Corporation Ltd., Melbourne	5.11 Mill. A $	–
First New Zealand International Ltd., Wellington	–	–

Notes
1. The Deutsche Bank has a 97.2% stake in the Deutsche Ueberseeische Bank.
2. Through SFE.
3. The Dresdner Bank has a 98.3% stake in the Deutsch-Südamerikanische Bank.
4. Through Hypo-Bank International S.A.

Sources
Banks' annual reports for 1974 and files of the HWWA Institute.

b) FOREIGN BRANCHES OF GERMAN BANKS

End 1974

EUROPE

Commerzbank	London
Dresdner Bank	London and Zürich[1]
Deutsche Ueberseeische Bank[2]	Luxembourg
Westdeutsche Landesbank-Girozentrale	London
Investions- und Handels-Bank	London
Bank für Gemeinwirtschaft	London

NORTH AMERICA

Bayerische Vereinsbank	New York
Commerzbank	New York
	Chicago
Dresdner Bank	New York
	Chicago
	Los Angeles

CENTRAL AND SOUTH AMERICA

Deutsche Ueberseeische Bank[2]	Buenos Aires (Argentina)
	Sao Paulo (Brazil)
	Asunción (Paraguay)
Deutsch-Südamerikanische Bank[3]	Panama
Bayerische Vereinsbank	Grand Cayman

FAR EAST

Deutsche Ueberseeische Bank[2]	Tokyo
Dresdner Bank	Singapore and Tokyo

Notes
1. Through the Compagnie Luxembourgeoise de Banque S.A., Luxembourg, in which Dresdner Bank has a 99.9 per cent interest.
2. The Deutsche Bank owns 97.2 per cent of the capital of the Deutsche Ueberseeische Bank.

165

3. The Dresdner Bank owns 98.3 per cent of the capital of the Deutsch-Südamerikanische Bank.

Sources
Banks' annual reports for 1974 and the company files of the HWWA Institute.

c) REPRESENTATIVE OFFICES
OF GERMAN BANKS ABROAD

End 1974

EUROPE

Commerzbank	Madrid
	Copenhagen[1]
Deutsche Bank	Istanbul
	London
	Madrid
	Moscow
	Paris
Dresdner Bank	Istanbul
	Madrid
	Moscow
	Paris
Bayerische Hypotheken- und Wechsel-Bank	Madrid[2]
Georg Hauck & Sohn, Bankiers	London

NORTH AMERICA

Deutsche Bank	Toronto[3]
Bayerische Vereinsbank	New York
Westdeutsche Landesbank-Girozentrale	New York
BIIΓ-Bank	New York

CENTRAL AND SOUTH AMERICA

Commerzbank	Buenos Aires
	Caracas
	Lima
	Mexico[1]
	Rio de Janeiro
	São Paulo
Deutsche Bank	Bogota
	Caracas
	Mexico
	Rio de Janeiro
	Santiago

Deutsche Ueberseeische Bank[4]	Bogota
	Caracas
	La Paz
	Mexico
	Rio de Janeiro
	Santiago
Joint representative office of the Dresdner Bank und the Deutsch-Südamerikanischen Bank	Asunción
	Bogota
	Buenos Aires
	Caracas
	La Paz
	Lima
	Mexico
	Montevideo
	Panama
	Quito
	Santiago
	São Paulo
	Rio de Janeiro
Bayerische Hypotheken- und Wechsel-Bank	Mexico[5]
Bayerische Vereinsbank	Rio de Janeiro
BHF-Bank	São Paulo[6]
Bank für Gemeinwirtschaft	São Paulo

AFRICA AND THE NEAR EAST

Commerzbank	Beyrouth
	Johannesburg[6]
	Windhoek[7]
Deutsche Bank	Beyrouth
	Johannesburg[3]
	Cairo
Dresdner Bank	Beyrouth
	Johannesburg[5]
	Cairo
Westdeutsche Landesbank-Girozentrale	Beyrouth
Bayerische Hypotheken- und Wechsel-Bank	Johannesburg[5]
BHF-Bank	Johannesburg

MIDDLE AND FAR EAST

Commerzbank	Singapore[7]
	Teheran
	Tokyo[7]
Deutsche Bank	Teheran
Dresdner Bank	Teheran[5]
Bayerische Hypotheken-	
und Wechsel-Bank	Teheran[5]
Bayerische Vereinsbank	Teheran
	Tokyo
BHF-Bank	Singapore[6]
	Teheran[6]
	Tokyo[6]
M.M. Warburg-Brinckmann,	
Wirtz & Co.	Jakarta

AUSTRALIA

Commerzbank	Sydney[7]
Deutsche Bank	Sydney
Dresdner Bank	Sydney
Westdeutsche Landesbank-	
Girozentrale	Melbourne
Bayerische Hypotheken-	
und Wechsel-Bank	Sydney[5]

Notes
1. Joint representative office through the EUROPARTNER group.
2. Joint representative office operated by Bayerische Hypotheken- und Wechsel-Bank and Banque de Bruxelles S.A.
3. Through EBIC (European Banks' International Company S.A.), Brussels.
4. The Deutsche Bank owns 97.2 per cent of the capital of the Deutsche Ueberseeische Bank.
5. Joint representation through the ABECOR group.
6. Joint representation through the INTER-ALPHA group (comprising the BHF Bank; Banco Ambrosiano, Milan; Crédit Commercial de France, Paris; Kredietbank, Brussels; Nederlandsche Middenstandsbank, Amsterdam; Privatbank i Kjobenhavn, Copenhagen; Williams and Glyn's Bank, (London).
7. Joint representative offices operated by Commerzbank, Banco di Roma and Crédit Lyonnais.

Sources
Banks' annual reports for 1974 and the company files of the HWWA Institute.

APPENDIX 5

French banks abroad

Bank	Associated banks and Subsidiaries (S) (Number of branches)	Branches and Representative offices (R)	Participations
Banque de l'Indochine		2 + 1 (R)	Handel-Mij. H. Albert de Bary en Co., Amsterdam Banco Europeo de Negocios-Eurobanco, Madrid
Banque de l'Indochine; Banque R. de Lubersac; Crédit Commercial de France; Société Générale			
Banque Nationale de Paris	Intercomi-Représentant, Madrid (S);	3 + 4 (R)	Banque Africaine Internationale, Brussels; Société Financière pour les Pays d'Outre-Mer, Geneva
	United Overseas Bank, Geneva (S); Banque pour le Commerce International, Basel (S); British and French Bank Ltd., London (S)		
Banque Nationale de Paris; Crédit Commercial de France; Crédit Lyonnais			Banque Nationale d'Investissement pour le Développement Industriel, Athens

Bank	Associated banks and Subsidiaries (S) (Number of branches)	Branches and Representative offices (R)	Participations
Banque Nationale de Paris; Société Générale; L'Union Européenne Industrielle et Financière			Banque d'Investissements, Athens
Banque de Paris et des Pays-Bas	Banque de Financement, Brussels (S) Banque de Paris et des Pays-Bas Ltd., London (S); Banque de Paris et des Pays-Bas pour le Grand Duché de Luxembourg, Luxembourg (S); Banque de Paris et des Pays-Bas, Utrecht (S); Banque de Paris et des Pays-Bas, Brussels (S) (55)	9	Corporación Española de Financiación Internacional, Madrid
Banque de Paris et des Pays-Bas; Crédit du Nord Banque Suez et de l'Union des Mines		1	Banque Sud Belge, Charleroi

173

Bank	Associated banks and Subsidiaries (S) (Number of branches)	Branches and Representative offices (R)	Participations
Banque de l'Union Parisienne	Sociedad Hispaño Francesa de Cooperación Técnica y Financiera S.A., Madrid (S)		Banque Internationale à Luxembourg, Luxembourg; Banco del Noroeste S.A., La Corogne
Compagnie Bancaire			Unión Española de Financiación S.A.-Unifiban
Crédit Commercial de France Crédit Industriel d'Alsace et de Lorraine		1 + 1 (R) 1 (R)	Crédit Sarrois, Hamburg; Banque Mathieu, Luxembourg
Crédit Industriel et Commercial	Crédit Industriel d'Alsace et de Lorraine, (S) (2)		Société Générale de Banque, Brussels
Crédit Lyonnais	Crédit Franco-Portugais (S) (3)	30 + 4 (R)	
Crédit Lyonnais; Banque Parisienne pour l'Industrie; Groupe de la Cie. Financière de Suez; Worms et Cie.			Banco de Financiación Industrial – Induban, Madrid

Bank	*Associated banks and Subsidiaries (S) (Number of branches)*	*Branches and Representative offices (R)*	*Participations*
Crédit du Nord	Crédit du Nord Belge (S) (9)		Banque Brugeoise de Crédit et de Dépôts, Brugge
Suez-Group	Suez Finance Company (London) Ltd., London (S)		
Lazard Frères et Cie	Connection with Lazard Brothers and Co., London		
De Neuflize, Schlumberger, Mallet et Cie.			Unión Industrial Bancaria-Bancunión, Barcelona Banco del Desarrollo Económico Español, Madrid
De Rothschild Frères	Secons Continuation Ltd., London (S) together with N.M. Rothschild and Sons		
Société Centrale de Banque	Foncaltun, Geneva (S) Banque de Salonique (S) (3)	2 + 1 (R)	
Société Générale	Société Générale Alsacienne de Banque (S) (3); Société Française de Banque et de Dépôts (S) (3);	2 + 3 (R)	

175

Bank	Associated banks and Subsidiaries (S) (Number of branches)	Branches and Representative offices (R)	Participations
L'Union Européenne Industrielle et Financière; L'Union des Mines "La Hénin"; Worms et Cie.	Société Générale de Banque en Espagne (S) (3)		Nederlands Franse Bank N.V., Rotterdam
L'Union des Mines "La Hénin"	Rembours en Industriebank N.V., Amsterdam (S); British and Continental Banking Company Ltd., London (S)		
L'Union des Mines "La Hénin"; Worms et Cie.			Banque du Bénélux, Antwerp

NORTH AMERICA

Bank	Associated banks and Subsidiaries (S) (Number of branches)	Branches and Representative offices (R)	Participations
Banque de l'Indochine		1 (R)	
Banque Nationale de Paris		1 + 2 (R)	French-American Banking Corporation, New York
Banque Nationale de Paris; Banque de l'Union Parisienne	Société Financière pour le Commerce et l'Industrie (S.F.C.I.) Ltd., (S) (2)		
Banque de Paris et des Pays-Bas	Paribas Corporation, New York (S)		
Banque de Paris et des Pays-Bas; Crédit Lyonnais			
Crédit Lyonnais		1	
Groupe de la Compagnie Financière de Suez		1 (R)	Crédit Foncier Franco-Canadien (9)
Lazard Frères et Cie.	Connection with Lazard Frères and Co., New York		
Société Générale		1 (R)	

177

CENTRAL AND SOUTH AMERICA

Bank	Associated banks and Subsidiaries (S) (*Number of branches*)	Branches and Representative offices (R)	Participations
Banque de l'Indochine Banque Française et Italienne pour l'Amérique du Sud-Sudaméris (Participations held by Banque de l'Indochine and Banque de Paris et des Pays-Bas)	Banco Mercantil (S) (2) Banco Frances et Italiano para a América do Sul S.A. (S) (25)	13	
Banque Nationale de Paris	World Banking Corporation Ltd., (Bahamas); Banco del Atlantico, Mexico (S); Banco Fiduciario de Panamá – Panamá Bank and Trust Co. (S) (2); Banco español y territorial – Union de Bancos des Uruguay, Montevideo	6 + 6 (R)	
Banque de Paris et des Pays-Bas			Banco Nacional de México, Mexico; Credito Bursatil, Mexico
Banque de l'Union Parisienne			Banque Hypothécaire Franco-Argentine, Buenos Aires

CENTRAL AND SOUTH AMERICA

Bank	Associated banks and Subsidiaries (S) (Number of branches)	Branches and Representative offices (R)	Participations
Crédit Lyonnais	Banco Frances e Brasileiro (19); Banco de Lima (3)	3 (R)	
Crédit Lyonnais; Groupe de la Compagnie Financière de Suez	Banco Provincial de Venezuela (10)		
Société Générale	Banco Supervielle de Buenos Aires (S)	1 (R)	

AFRICA AND THE NEAR EAST

Bank	Associated banks and Subsidiaries (S) (Number of branches)	Branches and Representative offices (R)	Participations
Banque Française du Commerce Extérieur Banque de l'Indochine	French Bank of Southern Africa (S) (5); Banque Française Commerciale (S) (2)	3	Banque Marocaine du Commerce Extérieur Banque Sabbag
Banque de l'Indochine; Banque de l'Union Parisienne; Crédit Industriel et Commercial; Société Générale Banque Industrielle de Financement et de Crédit	Société Générale de Banques au Cameroun (3); Société Générale de Banques au Congo (2); Société Générale de Banques au Sénégal (3) Banque Industrielle de l'Algérie et de la Méditerranée (S); Worms et Cie. (Maroc) (S); Banque Industrielle Agricole et Martime (S)		
Banque Internationale pour l'Afrique Occidentale (Participations held by B.N.P., C.C.F. and l'Union Européenne Industrielle		33	

Bank	Associated banks and Subsidiaries (S) (Number of branches)	Branches and Representative offices (R)	Participations
et Financière) Banque de Madagascar et des Comores (Participations held by Crédit Lyonnais, Société Générale, B.N.P., Paribas)		13	
Banque Nationale de Paris	B.N.C.I. Afrique (S) (6); Banque Internationale pour le Commerce et l'Industrie du Cameroun (5); Banque Internationale pour le Commerce et l'Industrie du Congo (3); Société Congolaise de Banque-Socobanque (6); Banque Internationale pour le Commerce et l'Industrie de la Côte-d'Ivoire (3); Commercial Bank of Africa (3); B.N.C.I. (Océan Indien) (S) (13); Banque Malgache d'Escompte et de Crédit "Bames" (9);	10	Banque Commerciale du Burundi; Banque Nationale pour le Développement Economique; Commercial Bank of Africa

Bank	Associated banks and Subsidiaries (S) (Number of branches)	Branches and Representative offices (R)	Participations
Banque Nationale de Paris; Banque Industrielle de Financement et de Crédit Banque de Paris et des Pays-Bas	Banque Marocaine pour le Commerce et l'Industrie (14); United Bank for Africa Ltd. (11); Banque Commerciale du Rwanda (3); Banque Internationale pour le Commerce et l'Industrie du Sénégal (3); Union Bancaire pour le Commerce et l'Industrie (5) Banque d'Escompte et de Crédit à l'Industrie en Tunisie (2)	2	
Banque de Syrie et du Liban (Participation held by Paribas)	Société Nouvelle de la Banque de Syrie et du Liban (S) (9)		
Compagnie Française de Crédit et de Banque (Société Nouvelle)	Compagnie Française de Crédit et de Banque (S) (93)		

Bank	Associated banks and Subsidiaries (S) (Number of branches)	Branches and Representative offices (R)	Participations
(Participation held by Banque de l'Union Parisienne)			
Compagnie Parisienne de Réescompte		1	
Crédit Commercial de France	Banque Franco-Suisse pour le Maroc (S)	1 (R)	
Crédit Industriel et Commercial	Banque Commerciale du Maroc (15)	2	
Crédit Industriel et Commercial; Société Générale	Banque de Tunisie (23)		
Crédit Lyonnais	Banque G. Trad; Société Camerounaise de Banque (11); Banque Commerciale Congolaise (6); Société Ivoirienne de Banque (8); Société Dahoméenne de Banque (2); Société Gabonaise de Banque (2);	10	

183

AFRICA AND THE NEAR EAST

Bank	Associated banks and Subsidiaries (S) (Number of branches)	Branches and Representative offices (R)	Participations
	Banque Malienne de Crédit et de Dépôts;		
	Crédit Lyonnais Maroc (12);		
	Banque de Développement de la République du Niger (3);		
	Philip Hill (Nigéria) Ltd.;		
	Union Sénégalaise de Banque pour le Commerce et l'Industrie (3);		
	Nilein Bank (3);		
	Banque Tchadienne de Crédit et de Dépôts (3);		
	Union Togolaise de Banque;		
	Union Internationale de Banques (Tunis) (3)		
Crédit Lyonnais; Société Générale Crédit du Nord De Neuflize, Schlumberger, Mallet et Cie. De Rothschild Frères	Union Bancaire en Afrique Centrale	2	The Merchant Bank of Central Africa Limited (Salisbury)
	Banque Foncière du Maroc (S)		
	Compagnie Africaine de Banque (S)		

Bank	Associated banks and Subsidiaries (S) (Number of branches)	Branches and Representative offices (R)	Participations
Société Centrale de Banque	Société Africaine de Banque (S); Société de Banque du Maghreb (S) (25); Crédit Foncier d'Algérie et de Tunisie (S)	9	
Société Générale	Société Générale de Banques en Côte-d'Ivoire (5)	4	
Société Générale; Société Marseillaise de Crédit Société Marseillaise de Crédit	Société Générale Marocaine de Banque (3)	12	

Bank	Associated banks and Subsidiaries (S) (Number of branches)	Branches and Representative offices (R)	Participations
Banque de l'Indochine	Inter Ocean Investment Ltd. (Taipeh) (S); Banque Française Commerciale (S) (2); Banque Française de l'Asie, Saigon (S)	6 + 1 (R)	
Banque de l'Indochine; Banque Nationale de Paris; Crédit Lyonnais; Union Bancaire et Industrielle	Banque Etébarate-Iran (2)		
Banque Nationale de Paris Banque de Paris et des Pays-Bas		10 + 6 (R)	Banque de Téhéran, Teheran; Industrial and Mining Development Bank of Iran, Teheran
Banque de Paris et des Pays-Bas; Lazard Frères Société Générale		2 (R)	

Bank	Asscciated banks and Subsidiaries (S) (Number of branches)	Branches and Representative offices (R)	Participations
Banque Nationale de Paris Banque de l'Union Euro-péenne		7	
Crédit Commercial de France	Patrick Intermarine Australia Ltd., Sydney (S)	1 (R)	
Société Générale		1 + 1 (R)	

Source
Crédit Lyonnais.

APPENDIX 6

Participations of Japanese banks abroad

End 1974

Bank	Participations	Percentage of capital held
Bank of Tokyo	Bank of Tokyo Co., New York	75.10
	Nomura Securities International Inc., New York	5.00
	Bank of Tokyo of California, San Francisco	53.10
	Chicago-Tokyo Bank, Chicago	4.91
	Innocan Investments Ltd., Montreal	2.70
	Tohcan Ltd., Vancouver	48.00
	Ventures West Capital Ltd., Vancouver	5.94
Dai-ichi Kangyo Bank	The First Pacific Bank of Chicago, Chicago	98.80
Fuji Bank	Fuji Bank Trust Co., New York	100.00
Industrial Bank of Japan	Bank of Tokyo Trust Co., New York	24.90
	Industrial Bank of Japan Trust Co., New York	100.00
Long-Term Credit Bank of Japan	City Bank of Honolulu, Honolulu	10.01
Mitsubishi Bank	The Mitsubishi Bank of California, Los Angeles	100.00
Mitsui Bank	City Bank of Honolulu, Honolulu	15.00
	The Mitsui Bank of California, Los Angeles	100.00
Sanwa Bank	Sanwa Bank of California, San Francisco	100.00
	Liberty Bank, Honolulu	4.90
Sumitomo Bank	Sumitomo Bank of California, San Francisco	52.70
	Central Pacific Bank, Honolulu	13.70
Tokai Bank	Tokai Bank of California, Los Angeles	100.00

EUROPE

End 1974

Bank	Participations	Percentage of capital held
Bank of Tokyo	Western American Bank (Europe) Ltd., London	22.50
	Iran Overseas Investment Bank Ltd., London	10.00
	Banque Européenne de Tokyo S.A., Paris	28.53
	Bank of Tokyo Holding S.A., Luxembourg	80.00
	The Bank of Tokyo (Luxembourg) S.A., Luxembourg	100.00
	Bank of Tokyo (Switzerland) Ltd., Zurich	100.00
	Bank of Tokyo (Holland) N.V., Amsterdam	75.00
	Banco del Desarrollo Economico Español S.A., Madrid	2.00
	CENTROFIN Finanzierungs-, Handels- und Treuhandgesellschaft mbH, Vienna	14.29
	Japan Investment Consulting S.A., Paris	50.00
Dai-Ichi Kangyo Bank	Associated Japanese Bank (International) Ltd., London	25.00
	Dai-ichi Kangyo-Bank Nederland N.V., Amsterdam	100.00
	European Brazilian Bank Ltd., London	8.90
	International Mexican Bank Ltd., London	7.25
	International Mergers Service AG, Zurich	6.67
	Interunion-Banque, Paris	5.26
Fuji Bank	Japan International Bank Ltd., London	20.00
	Fuji Kleinwort Benson Ltd., London	50.00
	Fuji Bank (Schweiz) AG, Zurich	100.00
	Dow Banking Corp., Zurich	10.00
Hokkaido Takushoku Bank	Banque Européenne de Tokyo S.A., Paris	3.73
Industrial Bank of Tokyo	Rotschild International Bank, London	11.40
	Iran Overseas Investment Bank Ltd., London	10.00

191

Bank	Participations	Percentage of capital held
	Banque Européenne de Tokyo S.A., Paris	29.60
	Japan Investments S.A., Paris	20.00
	Bank of Tokyo Holding S.A., Luxembourg	20.00
	Industrial Bank of Japan (Luxembourg) S.A., Luxembourg	100.00
	Industrie Bank von Japan (Deutschland) AG, Frankfurt	75.00
Kyowa Bank	Banque Européenne de Tokyo S.A., Paris	3.73
	Bankhaus Ludwig & Co., Dusseldorf	10.00
Long-Term Credit Bank	Manufacturers Hanover Ltd., London	5.00
of Japan	Banque Européenne de Tokyo S.A., Paris	11.08
Mitsubishi Bank	Japan International Bank Ltd., London	20.00
	Orion Multinational Services Ltd., London	16.66
	Orion Bank Ltd., London	10.00
	Orion Leasing Holdings Ltd., London	16.66
	Libra Bank Ltd., London	12.00
	Multinational Orion Leasing Holdings N.V., Amsterdam	12.66
Mitsui Bank	Associated Japanese Bank (International) Ltd., London	25.00
	Hambro-Mitsui Ltd., London	30.00
Nippon Fudosan Bank	Banque Européenne de Tokyo S.A., Paris	3.73
Saitama Bank	Banque Européenne de Tokyo S.A., Paris	3.73
Sanwa Bank	Associated Japanese Bank (International) Ltd., London	25.00
	Sanwa Financial Service Ltd., London	50.00
	Sanwa Bank (Underwriters) Ltd., London	60.00
	Euro Finance, Paris	2.74

Bank	Participations	End 1974 Percentage of capital held
Sumitomo Bank	Japan International Bank Ltd., London	20.00
	Banque de la Société Financière Européenne, Paris	6.00
	Handelsfinanz Bank, Zurich	5.00
	International Nuclear Credit Corp., Zurich	9.10
	Société Financière Européenne, Luxembourg	12.50
	Sumitomo White Weld, Zurich	50.00
Taiyo Kobe Bank	Banque Européenne de Tokyo S.A., Paris	3.73
Tokai Bank	Japan International Bank Ltd., London	20.00
	Interunion-Banque, Paris	5.26

End 1974

CENTRAL AND SOUTH AMERICA

Bank	Participations	Percentage of capital held
Bank of Tokyo	The Bank of Tokyo (Panama) S.A., Panama	100.00
	Corporación Financiera Colombiana, Bogota	6.80
	Curaçao Tokyo Holding N.V., Curaçao	100.00
	Financilar Banco de Investimento S.A., Rio de Janeiro	27.00
	Financilar Credito, Financiamento Investimentos S.A., Rio de Janeiro	27.00
	Banco de Tokyo S.A., São Paulo	100.00
	Emprendimentos Tokyo S/C Ltda., São Paulo	100.00
	Interunion Antilles, Curaçao	0.55
Dai-Ichi Kangyo Bank	Banco de Investimento do Brazil S.A., Rio de Janeiro	10.00
Fuji Bank	Asia Pacific Capital Corporation Ltd., Bahamas	30.00
	Banco America do Sul S.A., São Paulo	14.70
	Banco de Investimento America do Sul S.A., São Paulo	35.00
	Companhia America do Sul Credito Financiamento e Investimento, São Paulo	30.00
	Companhia de Seguros "America do Sul", São Paulo	10.00
Industrial Bank of Japan	Banco Finansa de Investimento S.A., São Paulo	3.60
	Corporación Financiera De Valle Cali, Colombia	3.00
	Corporación Financiera Colombiana, Bogotá	10.80
Kyowa Bank	Banco Union de Investimentos, São Paulo	10.00
Mitsubishi Bank	Banco Mitsubishi Brasileiro S.A., São Paulo	40.00
	Cia Tozan de Cred. Financimiento e Investimentos, São Paulo	10.00
Mitsui Bank	Banco Bozano Simonsen de Investimento S.A., Rio de Janeiro	5.00
Nippon Fudosan Bank	Banco Intercontinental de Investimento S.A., Rio de Janeiro	15.00

CENTRAL AND SOUTH AMERICA

End 1974

Bank	Participations	Percentage of capital held
Sanwa Bank	Leasing Bradesco S.A., São Paulo	10.00
	Banco Bradesco de Investimento S.A., São Paulo	10.00
Sumitomo Bank	Banco Sumitomo Brasileiro S.A., São Paulo	100.00
	Banco Halles de Investimento, São Paulo	8.25
	Halles Financeira S.A., São Paulo	30.00

End 1974

Bank	Participations	Percentage of capital held
Bank of Tokyo	AEA Development Corp., Manila	6.00
	Arab Finance Corp. SAL, Beyrouth	10.00
	International Bank of Iran & Japan, Teheran	30.00
	Bangkok Tokyo Finance Co. Ltd., Bangkok	34.00
	Uban-Arab Japanese Finance Ltd., Hongkong	8.00
	Tokyo Finance (Asia) Ltd., Hongkong	99.93
	Tomafin Ltd., Hongkong	50.00
	Singapore Leasing International (PTE) Ltd., Singapore	10.00
	Singapore-Japan Merchant Bank Ltd., Singapore	24.00
	South East Management Ltd., Hongkong	30.00
	Bunaiputra Merchant Bank Berhad, Kuala Lumpur	7.50
	Magnum Finance Berhad, Kuala Lumpur	10.00
Dai-Ichi Kangyo Bank	Asian & Euro-American Merchant Bank Ltd., Singapore	11.00
	Asian & Euro-American Merchant Bankers (Malaysia) Berhad, Kuala Lumpur	5.50
	Asian & Euro-American Capital Corp. Ltd., Hongkong	11.00
	Chekiang First Bank Ltd., Hongkong	33.33
	Thai Investment & Securities Co. Ltd., Bangkok	10.00
	PT Asian & Euro-American Capital Corporation, Jakarta	8.33
Daiwa Bank	PT Bank Perdania, Jakarta	24.50
	International Credit Alliance Ltd., Hongkong	25.00
Fuji Bank	Kwong On Bank Ltd., Hongkong	55.00
	Asia International Merchant Bankers Berhad, Kuala Lumpur	15.00
	Investment & Underwriting Corp. of the Philippines, Manila	22.50

196

Bank	Participations	Percentage of capital held
	PT Mutual International Finance Corporation, Jakarta	6.00
	Thai Fuji Finance Co. Ltd., Bangkok	49.00
Industrial Bank of Japan	World Finance International Ltd., Hongkong	25.00
	IBJ Finance Corporation (Hong Kong) Ltd., Hongkong	60.00
	PT First Indonesia Finance & Investment Corporation, Jakarta	7.50
	Korea Development Finance Corporation, Seoul	3.10
Kyowa Bank	Morgan Guaranty and Partners Ltd., Singapore	10.00
	Genbancor Development Corporation, Manila	10.00
	Kyowa Finance (Hongkong) Ltd., Hongkong	100.00
Long-Term Credit Bank of Japan	The Development and Investment Bank of Iran, Teheran	4.80
	The Bookclub Finance and Securities Co. Ltd., Bangkok	49.00
	LTCB Asia Ltd., Hongkong	100.00
Mitsubishi Bank	Orion Pacific Ltd., Hongkong	20.20
	Liu Chong Hing Bank, Hongkong	25.00
	Thai-Mitsubishi Investment Corporation Ltd., Bangkok	40.00
	PT Indonesian Investment International, Jakarta	20.00
	Yamaichi International (HK) Ltd., Hongkong	5.00
Mitsui Bank	WMS Capital Corporation Ltd., Hongkong	30.00
	Far East Bank & Trust Co., Manila	12.76
	Investment & Finance Bank, SAL, Beyrouth	8.00
	Philippine Pacific Capital Corp., Manila	13.33
	Mithai Europartners Finance & Investment Ltd., Bangkok	19.00
	PT Finance Corporation of Indonesia, Jakarta	17.00
Nippon Fudosan Bank	PT Private Development Finance Co. of Indonesia, Jakarta	8.00

197

MIDDLE AND FAR EAST

End 1974

Bank	Participations	Percentage of capital held
Saitama Bank	Saitama Union International (Hong Kong) Ltd., Hongkong	51.00
Sanwa Bank	Dariush Bank, Teheran	2.00
	Philippine Pacific Capital Corporation, Manila	13.33
	Aizal Commercial Banking Corp., Manila	10.00
	Baring Sanwa Multinational Ltd., Hongkong	40.00
	Bangkok Nomura International Securities Ltd., Bangkok	10.00
	Singapore Nomura Merchant Banking Ltd., Singapore	20.00
	UBAN-Arab Japanese Finance Ltd., Hongkong	8.00
	Inter Pacific Financial Corporation, Jakarta	41.00
	PT Bank Bali, Jakarta	n.a.
	Pertanian Baring Sanwa Multinational BHD, Kuala Lumpur	16.00
	DBS Daiwa Securities International Ltd., Singapore	10.00
Sumitomo Bank	Sumitomo and East Asia Ltd., Hongkong	40.00
	Merchant Investment Corporation, Jakarta	34.00
	Union Bank of SAL, Beyrouth	5.00
Taiyo Kobe Bank	Taiyo Kobe Finance Hong Kong Ltd., Hongkong	100.00
Tokai Bank	Commercial Bank of Hong Kong, Hongkong	10.00
	Genbancor Development Corporation, Manila	10.00
	Bangkok First Tokai Co. Ltd., Bangkok	30.00

AUSTRALASIA AND THE PACIFIC

End 1974

Bank	Participations	Percentage of capital held
Bank of Tokyo	Partnership Pacific Ltd., Sydney	33.33
	Beneficial Finance Corporation Ltd., Adelaide	20.00
	Burns Philip and International Trustee Co Ltd., Vila, New Hebrides	5.48
Dai-Ichi Kangyo Bank	Development Finance Corporation Ltd., Sydney	2.33
	Japan Australia Investment Co. Ltd., Sydney	20.00
	MBC International Ltd., Melbourne	10.00
	The New Hebrides Trust Co. Ltd., Vila, New Hebrides	10.00
Fuji Bank	Euro Pacific Finance Corporation Ltd., Melbourne	15.00
	Commercial Pacific Trust Co. Ltd., New Hebrides	12.50
Industrial Bank of Japan	Australian United Corporation, Melbourne	4.00
Mitsubishi Bank	Australian International Finance Corporation Ltd., Melbourne	20.00
Mitsui Bank	Tricontinental Corporation, Melbourne	12.00
	Burns Philip and International Trust Co. Ltd., Vila, New Hebrides	4.60
Sanwa Bank	Commercial Continental (Securities) Ltd., Sydney	19.30
	Commercial Continentental Ltd., Sydney	19.30
	The New Hebrides Trust Co. Ltd., Vila, New Hebrides	10.00
Sumitomo Bank	Sumitomo Australian Development Pty, Sydney	10.00
	Pacific International Trust Co., Vila, New Hebrides	20.00
Tokai Bank	Patric Intermarine (Australia) Ltd., Sydney	10.00

Source
Ichiro Takeuchi: Japanese banks overseas in 1974, in *Euromoney* (April 1975) p. 63 f.

199

BIBLIOGRAPHY

Books, and articles from books and magazines

Adams, T.F.M.; Hoshii, Iwao
   A Financial History of the New Japan, Palo Alto 1972

Asami, Tadahiro
   Der japanische Kapitalmarkt, die jüngsten Entwicklungen, in
   Finanzierung und Entwicklung, Vol. 9 (1972) No. 4, p. 50-54

Attwood, T.M.
   Singapore—The Asian Dollar Market, in *Euromoney* (March 1972) p.
   56-58

Baehring, Bernd
   Luxemburg—"An ally of the City", in *The Banker,* Vol. 123, No.
   568(June 1973) p. 580-584
   Weltfinanz im Fernen Osten, Frankfurt/Main 1973

The Banker Research Unit (Publ.)
   Who owns what in world banking 1974-75, London, September 1974
Bennett, Alfred R.
   American Commercial Banking: The Changing Scene, in *Lloyds Bank
   Review,* No. 101 (July 1971) p. 39-53

Boeck, Klaus
   Entwicklung und Förderung der britischen Direktinvestitionen, in
   Hans-Eckart Scharrer (ed.): *Förderung privater Direktinvestitionen,*
   Hamburg 1972, p. 229-319

Brunsden, Peter
   The Edge Act in US Banking, in *The Banker,* Vol. 123, No. 564
   (February 1973) p. 143-152

The money markets: A guide, in *The Banker,* Vol. 123, No. 571 (September 1973) p. 1031-1039

Campbell, Mary
Brussels—Service Centre for European Finance, in *The Banker,* Vol. 122, No. 554 (April 1972) p. 481-491
The Multinational Banking Framework, in *The Banker,* Vol. 121, No. 544 (June 1971) p. 628-639

Carmoy, Hervé de
Foreign Banks, in *The Banker,* Vol. 123, No. 563 (January 1973) p. 54-60

Clarke, William M.
The City's foreign business: role of the banks, in *Euromoney,* (December 1972) p. 13-15

Cooley, Richard P.
Foreign Bank Activity in the United States, Association of Reserve City Banking, Annual Meeting, Boca Raton, Florida, April 10, 1973, p. 1-22

Davidson, Robert L.
Foreign banks—a crowded road to Tokyo, in *The Banker,* Vol. 123, No. 569 (July 1973) p. 807-813

Denham, G.; Chaloner, E.
The prospects for foreign financial institutions in Japan, in *Euromoney,* Survey: Japan—the rising force in international banking (March 1973), p. 25-28

Dormanns, Albert
Deutsche Banken im Ausland, in *Bank-Betrieb,* Vol. 10 (1970) No. 1, p. 3-8
Japans Banken an der Schwelle zu einer neuen Entwicklung, in *Bank-Betrieb,* Vol. 13 (1973) No. 3, p. 84-88

Drumwright, J.R.
Foreign banks grow despite funding problems, in *Euromoney,* Survey: International banking in Japan—a survey (March 1974) p. 29-32

Ferrari, Alberto
New ways of international cooperation in banking, in *Banking in a Changing World,* Lectures and Proceedings at the 24th International Banking Summer School held at Chianciano, Rome, May 1971, p. 67-97

Fournier, Henri
Frankreich, in *Blätter für Genossenschaftswesen,* Sonderausgabe: Kreditwesen — Entwicklungstendenzen in acht Ländern, Vol. 117 (1971) No. 19/20, p. 369-377.

Fry, Richard
A brisk awaking, in *The Banker,* Vol. 123, No. 563 (January 1973) p. 41-43

202

Hongkong aftermath and prospect, in *The Banker,* Vol. 123, No. 568 (June 1973) p. 557-560

The financial 'miracle' is still to come, in *The Banker,* Vol. 121, No. 545 (July 1971) p. 782-785

Glow, Gottfried
Luxemburg als Finanz- und Bankplatz, in *Österreichisches Bank-Archiv,* Vol. 20 (1972) No. 12, p. 434-439

Gordon, Cadogan A.
British Banking in New York, in *The Banker,* Vol. 119, No. 521 (July 1969) p. 673-677

Grisius, Henri
An der Börse werden fast 600 Euroanleihen notiert, in Ministère d'Etat, Service Information et Presse: *Bulletin de Documentation* (1973) No. 1, p. 12-14

Guttentag, Jack M.; Herman, Edward S.
Banking structure and performance, New York 1967

Haubold, Dietmar
Direktinvestitionen und Zahlungsbilanz, Hamburg 1972

Entwicklung und Förderung der amerikanischen Direktinvestitionen, in Hans-Eckart Scharrer (ed.): *Förderung privater Direktinvestitionen,* Hamburg 1972, p. 89-227

Hein, Manfred
Strukturanalysen ausländischer Bankensysteme: Großbritannien, in Erich Thiess (ed.): *Schriftenreihe des Instituts für Bank und Kreditwirtschaft der Freien Universität Berlin,* No. 1, Frankfurt/Main 1967

Holthus, Manfred
Entwicklung und Förderung der japanischen Direktinvestitionen, in Hans-Eckart Scharrer, (ed.): *Förderung privater Direktinvestitionen,* Hamburg 1972, p. 399-467

Hottinguer, Rudolphe
International business, in *The Banker,* Vol. 123, No. 563 (January 1973) p. 53-54

Iklé, Max
Die Schweiz als internationaler Kapitalmarkt, in R.F. Behrendt, W. Müller, H. Sieber, M. Weber (eds.): *Strukturwandlungen der Schweizerischen Wirtschaft und Gesellschaft,* Bern 1962

Swiss invisible earnings, in *The Banker,* Vol. 123, No. 564 (February 1973) p. 186-191

Israel, Edmond
Clearing-Stelle erleichtert den Handel mit Effekten, Cedel verwahrt Euro-Bonds im Wert von vier Milliarden Dollar, in Ministère d'Etat, Service Information et Presse: *Bulletin de Documentation* (1973) No. 1, p. 10-11

Jungnickel, Rolf; Koopmann, Georg
Im Ausland auf dem Vormarsch, in *Manager Magazin*, No. 12 (1973) p. 116-121

Wie multinational sind die deutschen Unternehmen? in *Wirtschaftsdienst*, Vol. 52 (1972) No. 4, p. 191-195

Jungnickel, Rolf; Koopmann, Georg; Matthies, Klaus; Sutter, Rolf (Publ. by Manfred Holthus)
Die deutschen multinationalen Unternehmen, Frankfurt/Main 1974

Kathe, Raymond A.
Asiadollar Market, Benefits in Lending, in *Far Eastern Economic Review*, Vol. 80 (1973) No. 14, p. 35-37

Klopstock, Fred H.
Foreign Banks in the United States: Scope and Growth of Operations, in *Federal Reserve Bank of New York, Monthly Review*, Vol. 53 (1973) No. 6, p. 140-154

Komatsubara, T.
Overseas activities of japanese banks, in *The Banker*, Vol. 120, No. 531 (May 1970) p. 472-477

Krägenau, Henry
Entwicklung und Förderung der deutschen Direktinvestitionen, in Hans-Eckart Scharrer (ed.): *Förderung privater Direktinvestitionen*, Hamburg 1972, p. 469-631

Krebs, Ward C.
Foreign Banks in California—and the US, in *Euromoney* (December 1973) p. 60-63

Küppers, Bernd
Zur Bankenkonzentration in Großbritannien, in *Sparkasse*, Vol. 85 (1968) No. 10, p. 155-159

Lang, R.
Das Emissionsgeschäft in der Schweiz und im Ausland, in *Schweizerische Kreditanstalt: Bulletin*, Vol 79 (April/May 1973) p. 10-11

Ling, Mary
Will the British banks confront, compete or co-operate?, in *Commerce International*, The Journal of the London Chamber of Commerce and Industry, No. 1401 (January 1973) p. 10-15

204

Marcille, Yves
Les relations bancaires Franco-Belges, in *Revue Banque,* No. 315 (February 1973) p. 111-115

Mason, Sandra
Merchant banking today and in future, in *Journal of Business Finance,* Vol. 3 (1971) No. 4, p. 4-28

Mayer, Otto G.
Direktinvestitionen und Wachstum, Hamburg 1973

Muhlen, Ernest
Das Großherzogtum sprengt engräumige Kapitalmärkte, in Ministère d'Etat, Service Information et Presse: *Bulletin de Documentation* (1973) No. 1, p. 8-10

Neubronner, Ernst
Die Europäischen Finanzzentren, in *Blätter für Genossenschaftwesen,* Vol. 118 (1972) No. 24, p. 405-409

Nishiyama, Seiichi
The Japanese money market and capital flows, in *Euromoney,* Survey: Japan — the rising force in international banking (March 1973) p. 21-23

Pringle, Robin
Banking in Britain, London 1973

Radice, Jonathan
French Banking, in *The Banker,* Vol. 123, No. 563 (January 1973) p. 51-53

Reinhardt, E.
Switzerland — International Finance Center, Publ. by Swiss Credit Bank, Zürich 1966

Saldern, Sabine von
Internationaler Vergleich der Direktinvestitionen wichtiger Industrieländer, HWWA-Report No. 15, Hamburg 1973

Schäfer, Alfred
Die internationalen Kapitalmärkte aus schweizerischer Sicht, in *Zeitschrift für das gesamte Kreditwesen,* Vol. 22 (1969) No. 24, p. 1157-1158

Scharrer, Hans-Eckart (ed.)
Förderung privater Direktinvestitionen, Hamburg 1972

Scheffer, Cees F.
The present and future of the London merchant banks, SUERF Series 15 A, Tilburg 1974

Schmidt, Hartmut
Vereinigte Staaten von Amerika, in *Blätter für Genossenschaftswesen,* Vol. 117 (1971) No. 19/20, p. 416/424

Schmidt, Karl-Georg
Deutsche Banken in Entwicklungsländern, in *Bank-Betrieb*, Vol. 6 (1966) No. 9, p. 225-230

Schrott, Franz
Finanzplätze in aller Welt, Singapur, in *Zeitschrift für das gesamte Kreditwesen*, Vol. 26 (1973) No. 23, p. 1154-1156

Shinoki, Tatsuo
Changes in the Tokyo capital market—and its problems, in *Euromoney*, Survey: Japan—the rising force in international banking (March 1973) p. 15-19

Stein, Jürgen
Multinationale Banken werden immer vielseitiger, in *Bank-Betrieb*, Vol. 12 (1972) No. 4, p. 151-156

Takeuchi, Ichiro
Expansion of Japanese banking abroad, in *Euromoney*, Survey: Japan—the rising force in international banking (March 1973) p. 2-9

Japanese Banks Overseas, in *The Bankers' Magazine*, Vol. 204 (1967) No. 1483, p. 173-177

Japanese banks overseas in 1973, in *Euromoney*, Survey: International banking in Japan—a survey (March 1974) p. 7-15

Japanese banks overseas in 1974, in *Euromoney* (April 1975) p. 63-69

Tonello, Antonio
Foreign Banks in Italy, in *The Banker*, Vol. 121, No. 545 (July 1971) p. 822-828

Urcinoli, J. Arthur
The U.S. capital market as a source of funds for international issuers, in *Euromoney* (September 1973) p. 4-11

Venu, S.
A Note on the Asian Dollar Market, in *The Bankers' Magazine*, Vol. 216, No. 1514 (September 1973) p. 117-119

Weidenhammer, Robert M.; Adelberger, Otto L.
Das Bank- und Börsenwesen in den USA, Taschenbücher für Geld, Bank und Börse, No. 32, Frankfurt 1966

Wendt, Otto
Finanzplätze in aller Welt, Hongkong, in *Zeitschrift für das gesamte Kreditwesen*, Vol. 26 (1973) No. 23, p. 1146

Williamson, George
Finanzplatz London, in Schweizerische Kreditanstalt; *Bulletin*, Vol. 78 (July 1972) p. 17-19

Zimmermann, Fritz
Auslandsbanken in der Schweiz, in *Der Schweizer Treuhänder*, Vol. 47 (1973) No. 2, p. 36-40

Anonymous articles

Attention, the Ides of March, International Banking, in *The Economist*, Survey: The year of the barriers, an international banking survey, Vol. 246 (1973) No. 6753, p. 37-43

Developments in Eurodollar business, in *The Banker*, Vol. 122, No. 561 (November 1972) p. 1433-1437

Foreign banks in France, in *The Banker*, Vol. 123, No. 563 (January 1973) p. 79-85

Interview M. Giscard d'Estaing, in *The Banker*, Vol. 123, No. 563 (January 1973) p. 44-49

Merchant banks, Paribas on display, in *The Economist*, Vol. 247, No. 6773 (June 1973) p. 106

Multinationalization of Japanese Firms — (4), Banking & Securities, in *The Oriental Economist*, Vol. 41 (1973) No. 748, p. 20-26

Notebook Britain, US banks in London, in *The Banker*, Vol. 123, No. 567 (May 1973) p. 448-451

Overseas Branches of Member Banks, in *Federal Reserve Bulletin* (September 1971) p. 757-758

Recent Activities of Foreign Branches of U.S. Banks, in *Federal Reserve Bulletin* (October 1972) p. 855-865

The Asian Dollar Market in Singapore, in *Moscow Narodny Bank: Quarterly Review*, Vol. 23, No. 4 (Winter 1972/73) p. 23-27

The "big four" part company, in *The Banker*, Vol. 123, No. 570 (August 1973) p. 935-943

The record of the past 12 months, in *The Banker*, Vol. 122, No. 561 (November 1972) p. 1453-1509

Publications of official organisations

Bank of England
Quarterly Bulletin

Board of Governors of the Federal Reserve System, Washington
Federal Reserve Bulletin

Bundesministerium der Finanzen
Finanznachrichten, No. 4/1973 (September 14, 1973)

Bundesministerium der Wirtschaft
Bekanntmachungen, in *Bundesanzeiger*

Central Office of Information
Die britischen Finanz-Institute, London, June 1971

Deutsche Bundesbank
Die Zweigstellen ausländischer Banken in der Bundesrepublik, in *Monatsberichte der Deutschen Bundesbank,* Vol. 24 (1972) No. 4, p. 21-32

OECD
Financial Statistics, No. 6, Tome I, December 1972

Newspaper articles

Aldington, Lord
Operation abroad from a home base, in *The Times,* London, No. 57842 (April 13, 1970)

Benckendorff, Paul von
Tokio könnte zum London des Ostens werden, in *Handelsblatt,* Survey: Finanzzentren in Asien, No. 238 (December 11, 1973)

Bendall, D.V.
Leichte Kavallerie – Britische "merchant banks" und ihre Rolle, in *Die Welt,* No. 118 (May 24, 1972)

Bolton, George
American banks spread world branches, in *The Times,* London, No. 56935 (May 8, 1967)

Campbell, Mary
A leading place in the international scene, in *The Financial Times,* No. 26095 (June 28, 1973)

Facing up to a time of change, in *The Financial Times,* Survey: Dutch Capital Markets, No. 26304 (March 5, 1974)

Widespread increase in international operations, in *The Financial Times,* No. 26190 (October 18, 1973)

Colchester, Nicholas
Dollar on the defensive, in *The Financial Times,* No. 25769 (May 30, 1972)

Cornwall, Rupert
Role of Paris in financial world, in *the Financial Times,* No. 26057 (May 14, 1973)

Dalby, Stewart
A centre in its own right, in *The Financial Times,* Financial Times
Survey: World banking XX, No. 26036 (April 16, 1973)

Dicks, Adrian
Latest results are surprisingly healthy, in *The Financial Times,* Financial Times Survey: World Banking XXV, France, No. 25774 (June 5,
1972)

Engelen, Klaus
US-Banken im Ausland sehr dynamisch, in *Handelsblatt,* No. 203
(October 21, 1968)

Foldessy, Edward P.
Branching Out – U.S. Banks Find Money in Offices Abroad, Foreign
Profit Gains Outpace Home Results, in *The Wall Street Journal,* New
York, No. 104 (May 26, 1972)

Fry, Richard
British banks with a stake in America, in *The Times,* London, No. 57477
(February 5, 1969)

Gooding, Ken
Consortia concepts, in *The Financial Times,* No. 26036 (April 16, 1973)

Gwinner, Christopher
Why U.S. banks come to London, in *The Financial Times,* No. 24529
(May 1, 1968)

Haeusgen, Helmut
Singapur wächst zu bedeutender Kapitaldrehscheibe Asiens heran, in
Handelsblatt, No. 220 (November 14, 1972)

Hahn, Rudolf
Konzentration im Kreditgewerbe, England I, Schritte auf dem Weg
zur Universalbank, in *Handelsblatt,* No. 77 (April 19, 1968)

Konzentration im Kreditgewerbe, England II, Rationalisierung ist
Trumpf, in *Handelsblatt,* No. 78 (April 22, 1968)

Ishida, Tadashi
Der Internationalisierung des Tokioter Kapitalmarktes steht noch eine
Reihe von Hindernissen im Weg, in *Handelsblatt,* Survey: Finanz-
zentren in Asien, No. 238 (December 11, 1973)

Kippenberger, Hanns
Nach acht Jahren Erfahrung kann man sagen, daß die Hauptgründe, die
zum Entstehen dieser internationalen Banken führten, auch heute noch
voll oder sogar in verstärktem Maße gültig sind, in *Handelsblatt,*
Survey: Banken International, No. 215, (November 9, 1971)

Kojima, Akira
Japans Kapitalkontrollen sind weitgehend abgebaut, in *Handelsblatt,* Survey: Finanzzentren in Asien, No. 238 (December 11, 1973)

Mauthner, Robert
Tough going in constant bid to counter inflation, in *The Financial Times,* Financial Times Survey: World Banking VII, France, No. 26036 (April 16, 1973)

Morrison, Ian
Retreat from the third world, in *The Times,* London, No. 58150 (April 19, 1971)

Proctor, Simon
First moves to set up abroad, in *The Financial Times,* No. 25189 (July 1, 1970)

Wicks, John
The gnomes of Zurich and elsewhere, in *The Financial Times,* No. 26095 (June 28, 1973)

Anonymous articles

Banken — Feine Töchter in Luxemburg, in *Wirtschaftswoche,* No. 15 (April 6, 1973) and *Nachrichten für Außenhandel,* No. 80 (April 24, 1973)

Banktöchter im Ausland unter der Lupe, in *Süddeutsche Zeitung,* No. 271 (November 24, 1972)

Clearing system, in *The Financial Times,* No. 25398 (March 8, 1971)

Die Präsenz der amerikanischen Banken im Ausland in *Neue Zürcher Zeitung,* No. 286 (October 18, 1972)

Edge Act Affiliates of Banks Grow and prosper, in *The Journal of Commerce,* New York, No. 22589 (December 13, 1971)

Enge Kontakte der Großbanken mit London, in *Frankfurter Allgemeine Zeitung,* No. 265 (November 14, 1963)

Französische Bankinteressen in den USA, in *Neue Zürcher Zeitung,* No. 175 (June 28, 1972)

Giscard hat nichts mehr gegen Auslandsanleihen, in *Handelsblatt,* No. 11 (January 16, 1973)

La Banque Nationale de Paris au Japon, in *L'Usine Nouvelle,* No. 15 (April 12, 1973)

Mammut-Tanker und Büromaschinen von Orion, in *Handelsblatt,* No. 15 (January 22, 1973)

210

Midland's International Role, in *The Financial Times*, No. 25591 (October 29, 1971)

Neue Etappe in der Reform des Pariser Geldmarktes, in *Neue Zürcher Zeitung*, No. 210 (August 4, 1973)

New Horizons Open for US Banking Overseas, in *The Journal of Commerce*, New York, No. 22842 (December 11, 1972)

New strength for British banking abroad, in *The Times*, London, No. 56076 (July 29, 1964)

Paris fusioniert zwei verstaatlichte Banken, in *Frankfurter Allgemeine Zeitung*, No. 105 (May 6, 1966)

Singapur, internationale Drehscheibe des Asien-Dollar-Marktes, in *Handelsblatt*, Survey: Finanzzentren in Asien, No. 238 (December 11, 1973)

Suez: Ein Kauf für Mutige, in *Finanz und Wirtschaft*, No. 13 (February 17, 1973)

The impact of foreign banks, in *The Financial Times*, No. 25954 (January 10, 1973)

U.S. Banking Overseas, in *The Journal of Commerce*, New York, No. 23091 (December 10, 1973)

U.S. Banks' Branches Overseas: A Statistical Record, 1965-1969, An annual compilation by the Federal Reserve Board, in *The Journal of Commerce*, New York, No. 22338 (December 14, 1970)

U.S. Banks, Scope for expansion overseas, in *The Financial Times*, No. 23328 (June 3, 1964)

L